RETURN TO SOUTH AFRICA

The Ecstasy and
the Agony

—◦◦◦◦—

TREVOR HUDDLESTON

Fount
An Imprint of HarperCollins*Publishers*

Fount Paperbacks
An imprint of HarperCollins*Publishers*
77–85 Fulham Palace Road
Hammersmith, London W6 8JB

A Fount Paperbacks Original 1991

A catalogue record for this book
is available from the British Library

Printed and bound in Great Britain by
HarperCollinsManufacturing Glasgow

RETURN TO SOUTH AFRICA

Trevor Huddleston was born in Bedford in 1913, and was educated at Lancing and Christ Church, Oxford.

After a period in Ceylon and India he was ordained in 1937, and in 1943 went to South Africa as Priest-in-Charge of the Community of the Resurrection's Mission in Sophiatown, and stayed in that country until 1956. He has been a champion of the black people there ever since.

In 1958 Trevor Huddleston became Prior of the London House of the Community of the Resurrection, in 1960 Bishop of Masasi, and in 1968 Bishop of Stepney. He then became Bishop of Mauritius and Archbishop of the Province of the Indian Ocean in 1978. He returned to England in 1983 where he continues to be active in the struggle against apartheid.

Available in Fount Paperbacks by Trevor Huddleston

NAUGHT FOR YOUR COMFORT

For
OLIVER TAMBO
HILDA BERNSTEIN
ABDUL MINTY

Comrades in exile

INTRODUCTION

Thirty-five years ago I wrote a book called *Naught For Your Comfort*. The title was a quotation from GK Chesterton's 'Ballad of the White Horse':

> I tell you naught for your comfort
> Yea, naught for your desire
> Save that the sky grows darker yet
> and the sea rises higher.

It was the story of my ministry in South Africa from 1943 to 1956 and predominantly of the recognition, early in that period, that the concept of institutionalized racism known as 'apartheid' was totally incompatible with the Christian Gospel I was ordained to preach and live by. It was and is incompatible because it was and is fundamentally evil. It is therefore irreformable. It has to be destroyed. I learnt this not from a study of theology or of politics or of sociology but from the people of Sophiatown and Soweto to whom I ministered. For I saw it not just as a destroyer of human dignity but as a blasphemy. And I still do.

That book is still in print and there is no need to repeat its arguments or to retell its story here. This book is a kind of postscript to the other, describing a visit made to South Africa in June/July 1991 and the impact that visit made on me after thirty-five years of involuntary exile. I have nowhere found it more perfectly summarized than in a short statement made by my friend – likewise a South African exile – Hilda Bernstein:

Despite the excitement, the reunions, the joy, I was left with a lasting feeling of anger. So the ANC is unbanned, Nelson Mandela is released, and we are back more or less where we were thirty years ago (the ANC was banned in 1960) except that Nelson was then forty-one, except there was no State of Emergency, no Terrorism Act, except that Victoria Mxenge, Ruth First, Joe Qali and hundreds of other anti-apartheid militants inside and outside South Africa were not murdered, except that tens of thousands had not fled into exile, except that four million had not been uprooted from their homes and dispersed in desert lands to fit in with apartheid policy, except that all the wisdom, the abilities, the energies, the constructive idealism of thousands of Nelson Mandelas had not yet been thrown away, confined to Robben Island, or killed and lost for ever. But if you are black you can now swim in the Atlantic.[1]

Since those words were written, over a year ago, a great upsurge of violence, starting in Natal and the Kwa Zulu 'homeland', has spread across the whole country. The process of negotiation has not even begun. Despite the repeal of basic apartheid laws like the Land Act and the Population Registration Act, apartheid is still firmly in place. And the international community, more especially here in the West, is totally confused and is in the process of pushing the South African issue off its agenda in order to concentrate all its energies and economic aid on the democratization of Eastern Europe and the nation-states of the old Soviet Union.

My purpose in writing this small book is to make a

positive contribution to the future peace of Southern Africa, and so of the world itself. And to make that contribution not by adding to the vast number of books exploring the complex issues underlying the present transitional phase in the struggle for liberation from apartheid, although that is inevitable. My object is, rather, to help the ordinary citizen in the global village of our world to share the responsibility for peace-making by a deeper understanding of this critical moment in South African history. For it is, above all else, a moment of hope.

1

I have stated on innumerable occasions over the past thirty-five years that I would not return to South Africa until apartheid was dead and buried. And I truly meant what I said. So why, in fact, did I go back on my own promise?

The reason was a letter from my old friend Walter Sisulu (one of those sentenced with Nelson Mandela to life imprisonment at the Rivonia Trial) in January which appeared to indicate that the African National Congress might invite me to a major conference later in the year.

Oliver Tambo, President of the ANC, was in London recuperating from a stroke in the previous year and I was in the habit of visiting him regularly as a very old friend. We had first met in Johannesburg when he was teaching at St Peter's School and before he and Nelson Mandela went into partnership in the first black law firm in the city.

Oliver had paid his first return visit to Mandela since going into exile in 1960 and on 4th March I wrote him a long letter asking him directly, as President of the ANC and as a friend, whether I ought to go back on my declared intention not to return to South Africa until 'apartheid was dead and buried', or not. I received the following reply:

My view remains, namely that you ought to go to South Africa in June, that is, you remain there before, during and after the conference. You, who have done so much work against apartheid from the time you arrived in South Africa to the present day deserve to be present at this conference, which takes place some thirty years after a period of enforced silence. Much of apartheid will have disappeared, thanks to the efforts of the liberation movement and other supporting forces. What will remain is something which will take very little effort to abolish, provided the right methods are used. This is why I consider it essential that you go to South Africa now, to ensure that what remains of apartheid is totally removed. I am waiting to hear from Walter Sisulu whether they think you should be invited as I suggest. I shall contact you as soon as I hear from him.

A month later I received the following letter from the Secretary General of the ANC:

Your letter of March 4, 1991, addressed to our President O.R. Tambo, has been referred to us for deliberation. After discussions with the Deputy President Comrade Nelson Mandela and chairman of the ILC Comrade Walter Sisulu, I was mandated to write this formal letter of invitation.

The National Conference of the ANC – the first of its kind in more than three decades – will take place on June 26–30 inst. This will indeed be a historic conference both in terms of the very important matters that it has to deliberate and consequent epochal decisions it will adopt.

In the light of the above, therefore, we think it is absolutely crucial that those stalwarts of the Freedom Struggle, such as you are, who have given their wisdom, energy and determination to the cause of liberation should, circumstances permitting, take their honourable and rightful place at conference. You, Archbishop Huddleston, together with the late Chief Albert Luthuli and Yusuf Dadoo, were the first recipients of the Isithwalandwe – Seaparankoe. The ANC and the people of South Africa have benefitted enormously from your selfless and unflinching devotion and contribution to our struggle for freedom, human dignity and social justice.

In recognition of your services to the people of our embattled motherland, the ANC hereby formally invites you to the forthcoming National Conference. You are invited *not* as an 'external delegate' or 'observer' or 'expatriate visitor'. You are invited as a *full delegate*. Besides participating in the Conference we would like you to visit major centres of our country to gain first-hand experience of the life and struggles of the people. We envisage that your visit should last for about a month.

We are mindful of your hesitation to apply for a visa to a government you do not recognise. Needless to say that you are coming to South Africa not as a guest of the racist regime, but as an esteemed guest of the Movement and the people. We shall nevertheless get in touch with the government to facilitate, with the least possible fuss, your entry. It is our intention to make your visit as easy as possible, mindful of the strains and stresses that a congested schedule may precipitate. Most unfortunately we are unable, at this point in time, to furnish you with a detailed programme. We are still consulting with religious, civic and other mass formations on the details thereof. We shall communicate with you as soon as these are finalised.

Finally we would like to apologise for the delay. The explosive situation on the ground is exerting enormous pressures on us. Please bear with us.

I replied, thanking the National Executive of the ANC from my heart for the great honour of inviting me to take part in the Conference as a full delegate and adding, 'I am also most delighted to feel that, although at the present moment in South Africa much remains to be done to bring about our total victory over apartheid, I could at least on this occasion, like Moses, see the Promised Land, and hope indeed to enter it if I live long enough. I still believe that apartheid will be dead and buried before I am ... I hope I have made it clear that I do not regard my visit as a cause for celebrating the end of apartheid but for taking part in the final stages of the struggle. Therefore I really do not wish on this occasion for any church celebrations of my return.'

I have quoted this correspondence at length because I want to emphasize in the clearest terms that I had no illusions about the danger I faced of mis-representation in the matter of my return. But, in addition, I also consulted all those in this country who were actively involved in solidarity movements supporting the liberation struggle. Above all the Anti-Apartheid Movement of Great Britain (of which I am President) and the International Defence and Aid Fund for Southern Africa of which I am chairman of trustees. Indeed I would be going back to South Africa in a true sense as the representative of those organizations and not purely in my personal capacity. So perhaps it is appropriate to explain their purpose and their role as simply as possible.

For the past thirty years and more the Anti-Apartheid Movement has campaigned with one purpose: *to end apartheid*. Starting in Great Britain in 1959 it has spread across the world and has become perhaps the most effective solidarity movement in this generation. It was a response to the appeal by Chief Albert Luthuli, in the year before the Sharpeville massacre, for a full-scale boycott movement aimed at isolating South Africa culturally, in international sport, and ultimately in all forms of trade and economic co-operation. Sanctions became the dominant weapon in mobilising the world community for effective action. In 1961 South Africa was effectively excluded from the Commonwealth; the United Nations General Assembly declared the South African regime a 'threat to world peace' and Albert Luthuli, President General of the African National Congress, was awarded the Nobel Peace Prize. In the following year the UN called for sanctions – in a vote that was carried year by year with huge majorities. As early as 1963 the Security Council imposed a voluntary arms embargo against South Africa, an act which had immense significance twenty-six years later in the final stages of the struggle for Namibian independence when South African forces were unable to match the sophisticated airpower of their Cuban opponents.

It is true to say that, following an International Conference on Sanctions in London, the world community was able to exert sufficient pressure on the South African regime to prevent the death sentences on Mandela and his colleagues in the Rivonia trial of 1964.

And so, right through the 60s, 70s and 80s the effectiveness of sanctions were proved by the support we received world wide. In 1977 the arms embargo was made mandatory, and in the following year the UN Security Council adopted resolution 435 declaring the South African occupation of Namibia illegal, and setting in motion the process which led to Namibian independence and full sovereignty twelve years later.

It is against this long and determined fight to capture the conscience of the world for a South Africa free for ever of the curse of apartheid that the sanctions issue should be judged, and it is this issue, fully debated at the ANC conference this year, which remains vital to the success of the peace process still. I shall return to it later.

The trial of Nelson Mandela and his colleagues was the reason for the creation of the Defence and Aid Fund by the late John Collins, canon of St Paul's Cathedral. He had visited South Africa in the mid-1950s and met members of the white business community, at their request, to discuss what in their view was an unjust attack – not least by people like himself – on the racial policies of the South African regime. Of course John Collins insisted on meeting also the black leadership and white liberals such as Alan Paton and Ellen Hellman. But with the arrest and trial of Mandela and the near certainty of the death sentence should they be found guilty, it became a necessity to provide the best legal defence that money could buy – and so, also, to raise that money quickly. At the London end of the operation

16

Collins set up an office in his own house in Amen Court. At the same time in South Africa, offices were set up in Johannesburg, Durban and Cape Town. Inevitably – as it did with the ANC and the South African Communist Party – the government imposed a ban on the Defence and Aid Fund, and for thirty years thereafter the Fund operated from London. But its scope widened, its operations expanded and its work for *all* political prisoners in Southern Africa (including what was then Southern Rhodesia and South West Africa) expanded too. A board of trustees was eventually set up to secure the future of what became the International Defence and Aid Fund for Southern Africa. But it was the far-sightedness, the energy and the total commitment of John Collins which brought about one of the most effective instruments for final success in the struggle against apartheid. The death of apartheid must mean a society based on justice. When history comes to be written it will be seen what an incomparable role in the battle for human rights has been played by IDAFSA. Its three aims were simple and practical. To *defend* political prisoners of all organizations and of every race, colour and creed. To *aid* the families of those in prison or of those killed or disabled by conflict. To keep the *conscience* of the world alive by all available uses of the media. I had the privilege of being chairman of trustees when John Collins died eight years ago until it was decided to return the work of IDAFSA to South Africa with the ending of the ban on its activities early in 1990. In my last full year as chairman our budget reached the £11 million mark, money which in fact could only be found by appealing to national governments and the UN special fund. But the method of transferring such large sums to South Africa when the banning order was in force has still to be told. Those who received the money would have been instantly criminalized if the source of aid had been identified.

So – together – AAM and IDAFSA are organizations which have played a magnificent part in creating the present situation and leading to the hope of a democratic, non-racial South Africa. I know that without those bodies and the commitment over so many years of all who have supported them, individuals, committees national and local, and their international outreach, this moment of hope would never have arrived. It needs to be said that at no point in their history did any British government contribute directly to our work. It needs to be said because it has a bearing on present policies with regard to the negotiation of a new constitution for South Africa and the influence, for good or ill, that the Western powers will try to exert on that process. The omens are not favourable, as I shall show later in this book. But for that very reason and because 'the price of liberty', anywhere in the world, 'is eternal vigilance' it is worth making the effort to understand what is involved for each one of us.

In making my decision to accept the invitation of the ANC to attend their conference I was certainly most conscious of my responsibility to the Church and especially to the Community of the Resurrection which had sent me to South Africa in 1943 and recalled me in 1956. My story in *Naught For Your Comfort* is not and could not be an individual history but rather – as at least I hope – the story of the work of the Community done, however controversially and inadequately, through me. The decision to recall me – certainly the most demanding test of the vow of obedience I had taken – led to much controversy over the years and also, in its effect, to my becoming an exile, a 'prohibited immigrant' in South

18

African government parlance, and to the loss of the South African citizenship which I had deliberately taken as a way of strengthening my position in fighting apartheid from within the country.

So, in fact, it was the authorities of my own Church who removed me from South Africa and from the struggle itself. At that time (1956) Desmond Tutu was a student. Today he is Archbishop of Cape Town and Primate of the Anglican church. I wrote to him as soon as I had accepted the invitation of the ANC and, fortunately, he was passing through London some weeks before I had to leave for South Africa. He told me he was uneasy about my return and followed our conversation with a letter in which he wrote: 'You should be here when we are *celebrating*. It would have been better had you come at the release of Nelson. There is a sombre mood abroad because of the carnage, and where will we be on the road to negotiation?' And he ended with the hope that I might be 'prevented from coming'. For me this was a real sadness, yet I fully understood and appreciated his concern – a concern lest I should be caught up in political acrimony and dispute. But it seemed to me clear that, having consulted everyone whose opinions I valued most I had to make my own decision. And with this Archbishop Tutu concurred and with typical generosity told me that, although he disagreed with that decision, I had 'the perfect right to make it.' He went further than this in a telephone call from Europe, where he was attending an important international conference, just before I left Cape Town for home, saying that his fears about the impact of my visit and my attendance at the conference had been unfounded.

Long years before all this I had written an article in *The Observer* in which I said:

The Church sleeps on – though it occasionally talks in its sleep and expects (or does it?) the Government to listen. And so the day draws rapidly nearer when the African Christian will be unable any longer to accept the authority of that Church: when its authority will be so blurred, so formless, so entangled in his mind with the authority of the state, as to be an intolerable burden. *And he will cast it off* . . .

That prediction, thank God, has proved entirely false, as I was to discover for myself throughout the three weeks of my visit. And Archbishop Desmond Tutu had certainly played a major part, together with Christian leaders of the quality of Beyers Naudé and Frank Chikane, to make sure that, when all other voices were silenced by banning orders and the implementation of the repressive apartheid legislation, the voice of the Church was heard and its message proclaimed to the world. It was for this that he, like Albert Luthuli, received the Nobel Prize.

In *Naught For Your Comfort* I had written, as I faced the reality of my departure, 'This is the end of a chapter. And I thank God I have had the opportunity of living through it. The least I can do is to try and obey His voice from the darkness of the years that lie ahead. And I am certain that, in the words of Mother Julian of Norwich, "All shall be well, and all shall be well, and all manner of thing shall be well" – for the Africa I love, the Africa of my heart's desire.'

On Saturday 22nd June 1991 – thirty-five years after my exile had begun – I set out for home. This book is the account of that homecoming and of the ecstasy and the agony of that experience.

2

> I give you the end of a golden string
> Only wind it into a ball.

William Blake's words are the best definition I know of the *purpose* of life; and the simplest. To talk about this in terms of 'vocation' or 'calling' misses out on two essentials – the freedom to take hold of life where it is, and the necessity, from beginning to end, to persevere in the work of living and refuse to let that work fall away through complacency. In other words, to lose one's sense of commitment.

My 'golden string' was given me, appropriately enough, at the moment when I arrived in Johannesburg, 'the City of Gold' or, as its African citizens call it 'Egoli'.

It could be said that in returning there after thirty-five years I was in some way unwinding the ball, going back to where I had started. I did not see it that way. Rather I saw it as a God-given opportunity to take a firmer hold on the string in the hope of influencing in any way I could those developments which would lead to 'fundamental and irreversible change' in South Africa. And I was convinced that the ANC Conference would have a profound effect to that end.

Early in 1956, just before I left the country, I was invited to a prize-giving ceremony at the Central Indian High School, Johannesburg. The school had a unique role in the struggle against apartheid education, for it was a private school established as a protest against the Group Areas Act itself.

The Indian Secondary School which had existed in the centre of the city was moved to the Indian group area of Lenasia and the Indian community refused to accept the racist implications of this action. They themselves not only funded the school but appointed a non-racial staff, some of whom were well-known Congress leaders who had been banned from teaching in state schools.

Amongst the top three pupils in his class was a seventeen year old Muslim boy named Abdul Samad Minty who received a prize from my hands. So began a friendship which has lasted, and deepened, to this day, one of the strongest threads in my 'golden string' and certainly one of the most precious.

Abdul and I have shared in many significant events, but none more significant than the founding meeting of what was called the Boycott Movement. It was a response to the international appeal from Chief Albert Luthuli of the ANC and the Congress Movement in South Africa to isolate the apartheid regime by boycotting all South African goods. Abdul had arrived in London in October 1958 and I had introduced him to Canon John Collins (with whom, over the years, he worked to establish and sustain the Defence and Aid Fund) and it was he who came to see me and invited me to address the founding meeting of the Boycott Movement on the 26th June 1959. My fellow speaker on that occasion was Julius Nyerere, soon to become First Minister and later President of Tanzania.

It became clear, after the success of a major rally in Trafalgar Square (addressed by Hugh Gaitskell, leader of the Labour Party), and a one-month boycott of

South African consumer goods, that more comprehensive work and more persistent education on the meaning of apartheid was needed. Hence the new name and the new campaigning organization to be known as The Anti-Apartheid Movement.

I left Britain in 1960 to become Bishop of Masasi, in Tanzania, when of course my friendship with Julius Nyerere continued to flourish, and Abdul worked with the Anti-Apartheid Movement becoming its Honorary Secretary three years later, a position he still holds. But his major contribution to the struggle came about in 1979 when, at the suggestion of the United Nations, the AAM initiated the World Campaign against Military and Nuclear Collaboration with South Africa, and Abdul became its Director. He had continued his education first at Leeds University and subsequently at University College, London where he had obtained the M Sc (Econ) in international relations and was offered a Fellowship by the Richardson Institute for Conflict and Peace Research in London: this research had special reference to South African foreign and defence policies and the effectiveness of sanctions.

All of this had relevance to my return to South Africa in 1991; profound relevance. When I was elected President of the AAM and, eight years ago, came back to England from my last job as Archbishop of the Indian Ocean, it was to Abdul that I turned again and again for the kind of expert advice I needed, most particularly on the issue of sanctions in all its complexity, and its vital relevance to the ending of apartheid. We travelled widely together. We met frequently in London or in the capital cities of those countries which supported the AAM and IDAFSA in keeping the conscience of the world alive to the need for urgency in ending apartheid before it led to inevitable conflict and fulfilled its evil potential as a threat to world peace. Abdul, who has represented the AAM at every Commonwealth Summit since 1961 (save the Emergency Summit on Rhodesia in 1966) has, in my opinion, greater experience and deeper wisdom than most world statesmen on the realities of South African government policies. Would that they were more ready to heed his advice and act on his counsel.

For me, when the invitation came to return home, the need was for someone to accompany me whose judgment I could wholly trust, whose reputation amongst the leaders of the ANC was unsullied and who would be willing to act as a kind of aide-de-camp in what I knew could be a very demanding schedule.

I had no hesitation in asking Abdul. And I have no hesitation in saying that it was the wisest choice I have ever made, and the most rewarding. For that journey has been the most significant journey of my life. Everything else is certain to be anti-climax.

*   *   *

In the opening paragraphs of my book *Naught For Your Comfort* I wrote:

> It is told of General Smuts that, when he said farewell to any of his friends or distinguished visitors leaving South Africa, he quoted the lines of Walter de la Mare, Look thy last on all things lovely, Every hour. Since I knew of my recall to England these words have haunted me . . . 'Partir, c'est mourir un peu', and I am in the process of dying: in the process 'every hour'.

I was not exaggerating when I added, 'The thing about

such a death, the quality of it, is to heighten the loveliness of what one is leaving behind.'

Certainly through the thirty-five years of my exile – through the many contrasting jobs I have been called upon to do, however challenging, however satisfying and fulfilling, however varied in their changing demands and the 'chiaroscuro' of light and darkness they created for me – the Africa of Sophiatown, Orlando, Pimville and 'Egoli' itself had laid its hold upon my heart for ever and would not let me go. It was the honeymoon period of my life which had taught me the meaning of love in such a way that no other time or place could ever supplant it.

And it was precisely this that made my return journey so full of apprehension for me. What would it be like to be back? What kind of a reception would I have after so long? Could I expect to be remembered by the survivors, and could I hope to remember *them* – the children who would now be middle-aged men and women, the contemporaries who would now be (at their youngest) nearly eighty years old? And after so many years of repression under a government which had tried by every means in its power to destroy their hope and had succeeded only too well in destroying generation after generation of their most gifted young leaders, how could I expect to find the familiar, marvellous vitality and warmth of those early days? I had a sleepless night in the plane wrestling with my anxieties, 'toss'd about, with many a conflict, many a doubt', until an African sun blazed through the windows, breakfast was served and eaten, and as we swiftly descended to Jan Smuts airport, the place of my departure, 'unforgettable, unforgotten', became the place of my arrival, and I braced myself for whatever lay ahead.

It was a Sunday morning. And for one of the few

times in my life it could not begin at the altar of God, 'the God of my joy and gladness'. For one of the few times in my life the love of God would reach me not through the Holy Communion of the eucharist but through the holy communion of human relationships restored and marvellously deepened by homecoming and welcome and joy. And so it proved.

We arrived so early on Sunday morning that it would not have been possible for people to travel from Soweto to greet me. Instead the whole leadership of the African National Congress, Oliver Tambo its President, Nelson Mandela its Deputy President, Walter Sisulu and many others had arranged with the television teams to have a photo-call and press conference which would be seen and heard in South Africa and worldwide. I had already greeted Mandela and the other Robben Island prisoners when they arrived at Stockholm on their first visit to Europe. But to meet them in Johannesburg was a different experience altogether. It took me back to those days before they went to prison, and to one day in particular, and that too a Sunday morning (after church in Sophiatown), when I attended my first major gathering of the ANC in a hall in the city and made my decision to commit myself to the struggle without reserve. That was in the early 1940s, within a year or two of my arrival. It was my Damascus road which converted me into an activist rather than an observer, a fully political priest realising that conflict with 'the principalities and powers' had to be a fundamental part of my pastoral ministry. And those who were on the platform at that gathering with me (I forget the immediate occasion, but it was one which certainly demanded the presence of the Transvaal leadership of Congress) were the same people who came to greet me at Jan Smuts airport forty-five years later. I find it impossible to describe my own emotions during that hour of reunion. Certainly their outward expression was inhibited by the television cameras and their crews, the journalists and their photography. But I was secretly glad of that. I could escape into my own flash-back experience of the day of my departure from the same airport. Much simpler then. Just one large open space for those embarking and just one airliner, a turbo-jet, on the tarmac. And the Bishop of Johannesburg, Ambrose Reeves: some of the brethren of my Community and a crowd (but not too large a crowd) of those Africans who could manage to be there on a working day, to see me off. I stood at the top of the gangway to wave goodbye, looking my last on all things lovely . . . Such thoughts mingled with the thoughts of the moment of home-coming, and the actual physical presence of Oliver and Nelson and Walter . . . but myself the sole survivor of that other moment of parting.

I was anxious to use the opportunity of television and radio to stress the purpose of my visit and to counteract any idea that I had come to celebrate the end of apartheid. I said that the ANC National Conference in the following week would be an historic event in every sense of the word; that with the peace process so seriously threatened by the apartheid regime's failure to remove the obstacles to negotiation and to curb the violence, I felt morally bound to stand side by side with the ANC, and by participating in the Conference to make what contribution I could towards ensuring that the peace process would get back on track and lead to a genuine united, non-racial and democratic South Africa. Then I was taken to a waiting car and driven, with Abdul, to our hotel in Johannesburg.

For security reasons Abdul and I and my ANC body-guard were given rooms in a part of the hotel not open to the general public, though connected with it. But word of my arrival had reached the domestic staff. A telephone call from room service said, 'Some of the staff used to live in Sophiatown and want to see you'. A delegation of women arrived at my door. 'Father, I used to live in Meyer Street and was at St Cyprian's primary school. You remember my father Isaac? Of course he is "late" (dead) for many years. Yes, we live in Soweto now, in Jabavu.' And so it went on; almost every day that I was there I would have a greeting from someone, possibly not even born before I left, but part of that marvellous Sophiatown community of forty years ago, and still part of it after being removed and dumped, their homes pulled down behind them, on the open veldt which has become Soweto.

Walter Sisulu had told me as we left the airport that morning that he would collect me after lunch and take me to a meeting in one of the suburbs. I had no idea what it was to be about. Abdul and I, with Walter, were driven to a place called Judith Paarl, a typical Johannesburg middle-class suburb. We were greeted enthusiastically at the entrance of what was obviously a church hall by one or two men with ANC badges. But when the doors of the hall were opened and we entered there was a sudden burst of noise, cheering and stamping and singing, and the whole assembly of about two hundred people moved to greet us. They clasped my hand, they gave me great bear-hugs all the way to the platform, and it was only when Walter called for order that they sat down and listened to his address of welcome. In fact he had brought me to the final gathering of one of the fourteen regional meetings of the ANC (representing Pretoria, the Witswaterand and the Vaal), called to elect its delegates to the Conference itself. It was the culmination of the democratically ordered process organized nationwide to give people at the grass-roots of the Congress their opportunity to make their own choice of representatives. And so it was for me an opportunity to taste democracy emerging from the decades of repression and to experience, even at that level, the enthusiasm and the total commitment of the people to a new South Africa. It was a taste of what was to come a week later when the Conference itself opened in Durban and the chosen delegates exercised so responsibly their democratic rights.

Looking down across the hall I was reminded of the protest meetings of the defiance campaign, of the resistance in so many different forms to Pass Laws and to the Western Areas Removal Scheme, to the Bantu Education Act and many other apartheid laws, which I had addressed in years past in the Odin cinema and Freedom Square, Sophiatown. And there too, I had had Walter Sisulu beside me. But then I had been part of the whole vital community, known to the people because I lived with them, walked their streets, entered their homes constantly. Now, as I could tell at once, most of my audience were in their early middle age and younger. They had never known me personally, nor seen nor heard me speak. And yet they had received me in exactly the same way as I had always remembered: not just with the respectful attention always paid to the elderly in African society, but with the wholehearted joy and enthusiasm of youth. No barriers existed between us, and no problems of communication either. I had not had time to prepare a speech, I simply spoke from my heart and they responded to the theme of my impromptu address, anticipating rather than hanging on my words.

Apartheid had been used by the National Party since 1948 to ensure by every means at its disposal and at every level of life the total separation by race of black and white. It had defined black participation in the democratic process as participation in cer.ain forms of labour – only. It excluded 87% of the land area of South Africa from black ownership. It deprived them totally of the franchise – and therefore from citizenship itself in their own country. And yet, in spite of all this, I was welcomed into their meeting as a comrade. 'Comrade' is their chosen title because it expresses the reality of a relationship that ignores the artificial barriers of race, class and hierarchy. If it has an ideological ring to it, that is because its true meaning has been overlaid by the manipulation of demagogues seeking power and control. 'The institution of the dear love of comrades', as Walt Whitman has it: that is my understanding of the word and why I welcome its use. It is 'the dear love of comrades' which must be recovered and made real in the reborn South Africa. And it was certainly that which was shown to me on my first day in Johannesburg that Sunday afternoon. More formally – but never as a mere formality – it was emphasized by dinner that night at the Carlton Hotel, hosted by Nelson Mandela and other ANC leaders in my honour.

It was perhaps significant, certainly so for me, that on Monday morning I found myself in the middle of a public demonstration outside the High Court in Johannesburg. In a city where such vast change has taken place since I left and where street names were virtually all that has remained the same, the High Court building, large, grey and dominating its surroundings, is exactly as it was. It is certainly a place I remembered only too well, standing in one or other of its many courtrooms, watching its daily stream of pass-law offenders being tried and sentenced, at one minute intervals, to a fine or a few days in prison for not having a valid pass and thus committing a criminal offence. The demonstration that morning was on behalf of three members of COSATU (the equivalent of the TUC) whose trial itself – certainly a political trial – was in contravention of the agreement between the South African government and the ANC, to aid the peace process by *not* initiating any new political trials, and thus making real negotiation a practical proposition.

A crowd with banners had assembled and the media were there with their cameras. I felt very much at home. On the morning of 10th February 1955 I had been present when, under the Western Areas Removal Scheme, on the orders of the Minister of Native Affairs, Dr Hendrik Verwoerd, the 60,000 residents of the freehold township of Sophiatown were forcibly evicted from their homes. I wrote at the time:

> On the broad belt of grass between the European suburb of Westdene and Sophiatown a whole fleet of army lorries was drawn up: a grim sight against the grey, watery sky. Lining the whole street were thousands of police, both white and black: the former armed with rifles and revolvers, the latter with the usual assegai. A few Sten guns were in position at various points . . . In the yard at the bottom of Toby Street, military lorries were drawn up. Already they were piled high with the pathetic possessions which had come from the row of rooms in the background . . . The first lorries began to move off to Meadowlands eight miles away to the west. The rain poured down . . .

The removal of Sophiatown was under way.

On the morning of 24th June, thirty-five years later,

I set off with Abdul and the BBC camera crew to visit the same place, no longer called Sophiatown, but Triomf (Triumph), to see for myself what I had often heard described in its new white surburban dress, but could never truly visualize. We drove along familiar roads, past the Country Club and Cottesloe and up the hill to Westdene. And there, crowning the hill, but so surrounded by new housing that I was not even sure that it *could* be the familiar square-built clock tower that had been the centre of my life for so many years so long ago, stood the Church of Christ the King. We drew up outside it, but a high brick wall now surrounded it, and when I tried the main door I found it locked. But at least, after many changes of use, it was still a Christian church and well preserved by a South African Baptist denomination. Everything else around me was unrecognizable. But I knew that I was standing at the top of Ray Street and that, across what used to be the school playground, but was now completely built over with tidy white suburbia, was Meyer Street where once stood the Priory of the Community of the Resurrection, and, facing it, the mission house built for our women missionary colleagues and named 'Ekutuleni,' the 'House of Peacemaking'.

In fact I soon discovered that virtually the only bit of ground *not* covered up with a new house was a strip of rough grass, untidy and contrasting with the neatness of the homes and gardens on either side, the place where our Priory had stood. Sophiatown or Triomf? I doubt very much whether the white residents of Triomf would object if their suburb reverted to its original name, since they are quite content that the streets their homes occupy are named as they always were. As I wrote so long ago, 'Sophiatown! The name has about it a certain historical

32

and almost theological sound. It recalls Sancta Sophia, Holy Wisdom, and the dreaming city where her temple is built.' But in fact it has a different, more romantic origin. A certain Mr Tobiansky, eight years before the outbreak of the First World War, dreamed of a suburb to be built on a rocky outcrop which is shadowed by the spur known as Northcliff. It was a most attractive site in every way, four miles from the centre of the city (though the city was still only a mining 'dorp' at that time). It had 'features' which set it apart from the flat, uninteresting area of the town. It could hold its own in natural beauty with Parktown and Houghton, soon to become the most fashionable suburbs. Like them it had iron-red rock for a foundation and for a problem in civil engineering. But Tobiansky bought that large, rocky plot of ground for his dream plan in development and in gratitude and admiration named it after his wife Sophia. As he pegged out the streets he named many of them after his children, Edith and Gerty and Bertha and Toby and Sol . . . And so they have remained. I have always had the feeling that that strong sense of Tobiansky family ties has perhaps rubbed off on the place itself, and may still *triumph* over the years of clearance, the uprooting of families and the destruction of the most vital, exuberant, human community I have ever known.

This sense of the history of the place was renewed for me the day after my visit in a quite remarkable way. The 'phone rang and I found myself talking to an unknown man with a strong and unmistakable Afrikaner accent. 'I watched you on television last night when you were visiting Triomf,' he said, 'and I discovered where you were staying and determined to speak with you.' What he told me would suffer if I were to attempt to write it verbatim. His voice was coloured so deeply by emotion and sensitivity as he spoke. Better rather to state as truthfully as I can the message itself and its consequences and to leave the rest to the readers of this book. It was for me part of the ecstasy which somehow was part of the agony of that return to the place I had loved more than any other in my life.

The voice belonged to a white building contractor who was completing a block of flats in Ray Street exactly opposite the church of Christ the King. He told me that the site had to be cleared of rubble that had lain there for twenty years or more: in fact it was probably the last major operation in the development of Triomf as a residential suburb. In the rubble he found a large, heavy polished granite stone and on it an inscription which read:

EKUTULENI
'He is our peace that he might create in himself
of the twain one new man'
To the glory and service of GOD and of Africa
September 9, 1928

The builder said to me on the phone, 'I thought I must preserve that stone and place it in the wall of the block of flats I was building. You see it was those *words*: they moved my heart so deeply . . . I can't explain, but it was the *words* . . . But,' he went on, 'seeing and hearing you on the telly, I knew that that stone belongs to you. You must decide what to do with it. I shall bring it to the place where you are staying and hand it over. And I hope you will not mind a photograph of us together with the stone.'

And so it happened. 'Ekutuleni: the house (or place) of peace-making'. I remembered so well that stone set in the outer wall of the building fifteen years before I arrived at our Priory. I remember so well my first morning visit to the remarkable women who pioneered the work of Ekutuleni long before the Community of the Resurrection came to live in Sophiatown and to build the new church and primary school. It was Dorothy Maud (a bishop's daughter) who inspired it all and chose the name for it, and no doubt wrote the inscription on the foundation stone which so moved my Afrikaner builder. The story and the lives of those pioneer women are woven into the story and lives of Sophiatown itself. But that story has long been told. Part of the ecstasy of my return lay in meeting, again and again, the men and women who had been influenced as children by Dorothy and her companions and those who had followed her down the years. For Ekutuleni reached out with its peace-making in such a wide area of compassion and caring that, even when the building itself became a heap of rubble covering for twenty years that familiar foundation stone, the work went on. I was told that the Ekutuleni committee had continued until now to raise funds for the same vital needs of those deprived still by apartheid itself of human dignity. And, by one of those extraordinary 'coincidences' which, for me, are more truly little miracles, the Ekutuleni committee had decided to build a small office opposite a new church on the fringes of Triomf (known in my day as Newclare) and, at that time the poorest part of the parish of Sophiatown. So the foundation stone will be incorporated in that new building, sixty-three years after its ceremonial incorporation in the old. It will be well guarded by angels and archangels, I am sure.

On that first morning of my return to Sophiatown, and on a second visit a day or two later, I realized that in truth I was seeing what has been Dr Verwoerd's strategy of 'grand apartheid' fully and ruthlessly implemented over the years until now. The Western Areas Removal Scheme was the planned precursor of population removals across the length and breadth of South Africa. It led on, inexorably, to the creation of the so-called Bantustans or Homelands as the answer of the nationalist government to the fears of its white electorate. It led on to the eviction and removal of over four million black Africans from their traditional homes and to the creation of a population in the squatter camps larger by far than the total white community of South Africa. It led on to a situation today in which those dispossessed of their lands – as the Sophiatown community were dispossessed of theirs thirty-six years ago – are claiming the right to return. And those four million are being told by President de Klerk and his government, 'If you want your land back you must pay for it'. I wrote this sentence in *Naught For Your Comfort*, and I see no reason to change it: 'Perhaps only the names of Tobiansky children at the street corners will remind people of its past. But it will be stolen property.' The only difference today is that that stolen property is nationwide and the peace process and the negotions yet to be begun will have to take it into account or remain still-born . . . Nothing could be further from the truth than to describe apartheid as a mistake. It was a policy meticulously planned and implemented and its purpose was to create a nation in which the majority of its people would be permanently excluded from citizenship on the basis of their race. Yet, so far, the Pretoria regime has not declared its repentance for apartheid, only its regret that it did not work, only its commitment to a 'new South Africa' which will be welcomed back to the world community.

Dr Beyers Naude, sometime Moderator of the Dutch

Reformed Church in the Transvaal, was deprived of his position and his livelihood when he declared in the 60s that he recognized apartheid to be 'sinful'. Tried and convicted of heresy and then subjected to banning orders until recently, he sums up the challenge in these words: 'How are we going to handle and heal the terrible injustice, the needless suffering and pain which apartheid has imposed on millions of our people? How are we going to help victims to forgive the torture that has been inflicted upon them?' And Bruce Evans, bishop of the Anglican diocese of Port Elizabeth, wrote in his diocesan newsletter, 'If the government is serious in wanting to eradicate apartheid (and I believe it is) then it is important to acknowledge that apartheid is and *always has been* wrong. It is wicked. In every respect it is sinful. With such acknowledgement there should be an apology from the National Party Government – Sorry, we were wrong. Forgive us.'

During my visit to Triomf I found myself at its furthest limit, driving past one or two houses on the edge of the open space dividing what had been the black freehold township of Sophiatown from its white neighbours in Westdene. I recognized the house of Dr A. B. Xuma, medical practitioner and one-time President of the African National Congress. He had done part of his training in the USA and married a black American wife. He had been forced to quit his home with the rest, but for some reason it escaped the bulldozers and is now, with a strong wall around it and a private swimming pool in the back garden, one of the more prestigious houses in Triomf.

The last place I visited on that morning of my return was St Joseph's House, its buildings quite unchanged, its function still the same as it used to be, its small chapel where I so often came to say mass for the Sisters who looked after the children, still the same place of prayer. The small 'rondavel' still stood a little apart from the main house, the home of the chaplain Father Michael Scott who was a frequent visitor to our Priory. Although Michael only spent six years of his ministry in South Africa (he arrived only a few months before me in 1943) he had been, as a young man of nineteen, working for a year at the Fauré branch of the Mission to Lepers and had done part of his theological training at St Paul's College in Grahamstown. After ordination in England he had gone to work in India for some years and it was there that he gained his experience of working with the poor and destitute. He was thirty-six when he returned to South Africa. I was just thirty. So he and I were exact contemporaries. 'But', as I said recently in an interview about him with Michael Worsnip, 'I think it would be fair to say that Michael was far ahead of me in understanding what were the real issues. He already knew the background. And I was very naive.'[2] Scott said of himself that he had come to recognize that there were 'two kinds of Christianity', one which provided 'a divine sanction of the *status quo*', and the other which was 'the religion which was the divine instrument of change'.[3] It was certainly this view which led Michael to launch his Campaign for Right and Justice, calling upon all the people of South Africa to 'stand together for what is just and right and to mobilize the widest possible alliance of the popular and progressive forces in the country' so as to secure certain defined and clear objectives. All this was in 1944 – four years before the National Party came to power under Dr Malan. Although Michael attempted to secure the support of the Anglican Church at the diocesan synod of that year, his efforts came to nothing and were in fact actively opposed by the then Bishop of Johannesburg (later Archbishop of Cape Town), Geoffrey Clayton.

'The Church of God', wrote Michael, 'cannot be content with defending attitudes, preaching sermons, and passing resolutions. The Church must be an instrument of change and redemption in the world. If it ceases to be an instrument of God's creative purpose and becomes an institution preoccupied with doctrine, church order and discipline, and identified with prevailing systems, the salt will have lost its savour and be fit only for the dung heap.'[4]

I have no doubt that Michael's influence and, more, his example of fearless intervention in the social evils and conflicts leading inexorably to the intensification of the struggle, had a great effect on me over the years. As I stood with the chaplain of St Joseph's Home outside his rondavel I felt the years fall away and I could almost hear that familiar voice and see that familiar ascetic figure. Once again I felt myself a survivor, but at the same time involved in the same struggle and the same conflict of nearly fifty years ago. But now I was within a Christian community inspired by a leadership which would subscribe to and not condemn the words of Michael Scott. In fact, the young chaplain who met me and talked with me about the St Joseph's Home of today had refused (as many of his white contemporaries had done) to do national service. He would not be conscripted, even as a military chaplain, to serve in an army used by the government to attack and kill black citizens – including women and children – in their own country. For this refusal he could have been sentenced to six years in prison. He was instead sentenced to a hundred days of community service and was serving that sentence by serving the deprived children – of all races – at St Joseph's Home. I am sure Michael Scott would have approved.

3

Two days after my arrival in Johannesburg I was invited to speak at the 23rd National Conference of the South African Council of Churches being held at the Lutheran Church Centre in the city. The fact that the SACC had not been founded in its present form until 1968, and I had left South Africa twelve years before, is itself an indication of the great change in the role of the Church over that period. In fact it would have been inconceivable in the 1940s and '50s for a meeting of this kind, a national conference with delegates from virtually every mainline church, and many others less mainline, to convene such a gathering. My memory takes me back to a seminal book entitled *Bantu Prophets* by Bengt Sundkler published some years ago, describing the two types of 'indigenous' black churches: those which modelled themselves institutionally on the parent missionary body and those which were in the broadest sense 'Pentecostal'. I, of course, knew both models because Sophiatown, being the vital community it was, had room for all its diverse families, not least Christian churches. What they had in common was their 'blackness'. The 'traditionalist' sects, like the Bantu Presbyterian Church or the American Methodist Episcopal Church and many others, had black leadership in their ministry but their forms of service were virtually unchanged from those of their white parent bodies. They had church buildings which, for the most part, were identifiable with those used by their white counterparts. Thursday afternoons, in Sophiatown, were a marvellous visual expression of their diversity. For it was then that the Mothers Union and their equivalent organizations donned their uniforms and came together for worship and discussion and social activity. The white blouses and black skirts of the Anglican women, together with the badge and the cincture, were matched by the red, the blue, the yellow, the purple of the other organizations. And the sound of hymn singing, full throated and enthusiastic beyond all description, breaking the restraining barriers of respectability, was heard all afternoon until, as the sun began to sink, the women returned home to prepare the family meal for husbands and children.

But the 'Pentecostalists' (I use that term with hesitation because it is an inaccurate blanket term covering a vast complex of religious sects and denominations) had broken away from the institutional, doctrinal, ritual and cultural forms of the traditional churches. This is not the place for either a theological or historical study, but Bengt Sundkler's writings provide exactly that information with empathy and scholarship. However, even in my day thirty-five years ago their presence in Sophiatown and Orlando, in Pimville and Kliptown – in what is today the vast 'township' of Soweto – added an unmistakable dimension to the religious scene. They were, and are, enthusiasts, with an enthusiasm which challenges the conformism and respectability of traditional Christian assemblies. They belong essentially to the open spaces of the vast African landscape, and the wide African sky is their backdrop. And this was true, and is still true, of the restricted urban areas in which they live and from which they go out to worship. Not for them any distinction in ministry between the sexes. Not for them the clerical clothing, the dog-collar and black suits of other ministries. White, with brilliant blues and greens, but flowing like Indian 'saris' are their costumes. There is a plentiful supply of mitres for both men and women for a headdress, and staffs made from branches of trees and shaped, often, like a shepherd's crook. And always their own kind of singing, unaccompanied, strong and vibrant as they move through the streets or across the open veldt or down to a stream for baptism by immersion. This is what I recall when I shut my eyes and think of the images of those years. And, like all memories, they are no doubt inaccurate. But for me, still, they bring back instantly a kind of joy I have experienced nowhere else. And, on my return after thirty-five years of exile, it came back to me again and again as I caught a glimpse of one of those processions in their white robes and heard their singing in the distance. So much did (and I am sure still do) the Pentecostalists contribute to the community where they live. In *Naught For Your Comfort* I wrote of Sophiatown:

> There are churches of every denomination and of almost every imaginable sect. There is one, for example, known as 'The Donkey Church' upon whose squat, square tower there stands in place of the traditional weather-cock, an ass. I would not know its real origin except that it is, I believe, a schism from the Methodist Church . . . Somehow or other that little donkey represents the freedom that has existed down the years in Sophiatown, and when I pass it, I metaphorically lift my hat.

It reminded me of the truth that G. K. Chesterton so simply and so profoundly taught in his poem:

The tattered outlaw of the earth
Of ancient crooked will:
Starve, scourge, deride me: I am dumb.
I keep my secret still.

Fools! For I also had my hour:
One far fierce hour and sweet:
There was a shout about my ears
And palms before my feet.

To which I added a post-script which I see no reason to
change even in 1991: even as, please God, negotiations
will begin in earnest for the peaceful ending of 'apartheid'.
I wrote 'Basically White South Africa has the same benign
or unbenign contempt for the African as man for the
donkey. Was it not Smuts himself who said once that,
"the African has the patience of the ass"?'

All of this is a digression. Yet I think it is an important
one, for, having had no experience of the South African
Council of Churches I found myself, at its National
Conference, speaking to a large delegate assembly, and
discovered very quickly just how fully representative it
was of the Church in that country today. I use the
word 'the Church' because I hope I have made clear
by what I have just written the amazing diversity of
Christian life that that term alone expresses. I do not
mean, of course, that that diversity is not at one level
still deeply divisive and can hinder or even at times
prevent effective witness and effective action. But it is
a fact. And the South African Council of Churches is
a response to that fact and for twenty-three years has
grown in strength and solidarity beyond all my own
imagining. On 24th June 1991 I found myself in the
company not only of delegates from all the 'main-line'
churches, the Pentecostal churches and the 'traditional'

break-away churches I have tried to describe, but of delegates who, in my day, literally never met each other and certainly never worked together officially. It would have been unthinkable in 1951 to hold a conference in which the Dutch Reformed Church leadership were delegates alongside the hierarchy of the Roman Catholic Church; unthinkable to see in the same hall a cardinal invited to contribute to the profoundly theological debate on major issues confronting South Africa, together with theologians in the Calvinist tradition, and each one committed to the same cause, defined in the title of this year's conference: 'From Egypt to the Wilderness: The Ecstasy and the Agony – challenge to the Churches in a time of Transition.'

The Secretary General of the SACC, Dr Frank Chikane, together with his executive council, had prepared the agenda for this year's conference with absolute regard for that title. It spelt out exactly the specific issues which had to be debated if, 'in a time of transition', there was to be an effective 'challenge' effectively met. If, in truth, having left behind the land of bondage, Egypt, the journey out of the wilderness would lead to the Promised Land. So – our programme told us – the first part of the conference would be devoted to 'The State of the Nation', and the major issues confronting us in mid-1991 were categorized in this way.

1 Obstacles to Negotiations. Have they been removed? Dispute about the Release of political Prisoners: Crisis about the return of South African Exiles: Repeal of the Pillars of Apartheid.
2 The Violence Problem.
3 The Sanctions Debate.
4 The Abolition of the Land Acts.

45

5 Marginalized Youth.
6 Repatriation Programme.
7 Standing for the Truth Campaign.
8 Dialogue with Political Organizations and the Government.

Part Two of the Conference was to be devoted to 'Ecumenical Solidarity Action'.

This agenda is as near perfect an exposition as can be found anywhere of the issues and the problems confronting not only the Church but the whole nation of South Africa in this time of transition. It was an agenda repeated in almost identical terms for the Conference of the African National Congress which was due to meet the following week. And it was repeated yet again a few weeks later at the Conference of COSATU (The Council of South African Trade Unions).

I attended only the opening session because my programme did not allow me to do more, but I heard the Secretary General's Report and it gives, in itself, an outstanding summary of the true meaning of those issues which have to be met if the negotiations between President de Klerk's government and all other organizations leading the struggle for the destruction of apartheid are even to begin. I quote that speech exactly as it was delivered.

The period covered by this report, since the last National Conference, was a very difficult one. On the one hand there was reason for great expectations and hope, especially with the agreements of the Pretoria Minute giving even a timetable and deadlines to remove obstacles to negotiations. In the same spirit the ANC suspended the armed struggle and moved on the

All-Party Conference which they hoped would lead to a Constituent Assembly, which in turn would be responsible for negotiating a new constitution.

On the other hand we were faced with escalating violence, fear, distress and a feeling of helplessness which caused many in the black community to shift their focus from the negotiation possibilities to the reality of death and destruction on the ground. The violence blew up their confidence on the future as they began to feel that neither the ANC nor the Government could stop the war. For them, if none could arrest the war the expected future then had no chance. This crisis of violence resulted in the ultimatum by the ANC to the Government to act decisively to curb the violence. If the Government failed, the ANC would then pull out of the All-Party Conference, and from negotiations on a new constitution.

This is where the theme of this Conference comes in: 'The Ecstasy and the Agony: From Egypt to the Wilderness'.

At the 1989 Conference we felt the existence of a confluence of factors which created a conjuncture that made a negotiated settlement possible. 1990 was a year of great expectations and hope for the future. Even if there was violence it was regarded as just birth-pangs, a sign of hope for the birth of a new country, a new society, a new people. But in 1991 it began to dawn on us that the birth-pangs might in fact be 'death-pangs'. I coined the word 'death-pangs' to try to express the idea of pains of death as opposed to the idea of pains of giving birth to a new life. It is a birth that kills rather than a birth that gives life. It is for this reason that resistance began to build up even against the very negotiation process. People began to engage in a struggle to save the new society from being stillborn, giving the system a further lease of life.

Like the Israelites, the Pharaoh is pursuing us. Some of us have been terrified by this fearful advancing army of the Egyptians. Some of us are beginning to feel that it would have been better to remain and maintain the old order rather than surge towards the new order. Some feel that it would have been better to serve the racist oppressors than to die in the wilderness. But we must say, as Moses said to the people: 'Do not be afraid, stand firm, and see the deliverance that the Lord will accomplish for you today, for the forces of violence (the enemies of your freedom) whom you see today you shall never see again, for the Lord will fight for you.'

The question or challenge that faces us as churches today is, what hope can we give to the people? Is there any hope for relief in the midst of this death and destruction? Will the Lord fight for us? Can the Lord cause the waters of the sea to return and toss the forces of reaction into the sea? Can the Lord drown them rather than let the hope for a new society be drowned?

Mr President, this is the context within which I have to present this report. I hope therefore that you will understand that I am as well part of this

A street in one of the 'shanty towns' (squatter camps) of Soweto in the 1950's.

Blessing a feeding centre for the thousands of children in the black townships of Johannesburg in the 1940's to the 1980's. The African Children's Feeding Scheme was founded by Huddleston in the late 1940's and its volunteer workers were always black and white together. *Credit: Steve Mornay.*

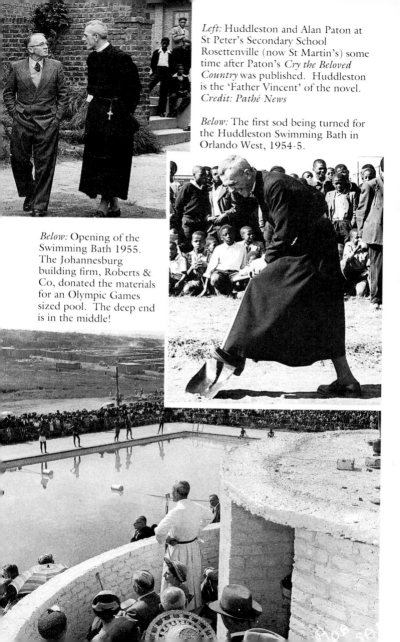

Left: Huddleston and Alan Paton at St Peter's Secondary School Rosettenville (now St Martin's) some time after Paton's *Cry the Beloved Country* was published. Huddleston is the 'Father Vincent' of the novel. *Credit: Pathé News*

Below: The first sod being turned for the Huddleston Swimming Bath in Orlando West, 1954-5.

Below: Opening of the Swimming Bath 1955. The Johannesburg building firm, Roberts & Co, donated the materials for an Olympic Games sized pool. The deep end is in the middle!

The Freedom Charter passed at the Congress of the People, Kliptown, clause by clause. At the top are the photographs of the three recipients of the Isitwalandwe Award - Chief Albert Luthuli, Huddleston and Dr Dadoo. *Credit: IDAF.*

The trumpeter is Hugh Masekela, the trombonist Jonas Gwangwa, and Huddleston stands next to Alan Paton. *Credit: IDAF*

One of the protest meetings organised by the ANC to oppose the removal
and demolition of Sophiatown. *Credit: Eli Weinberg/IDAF*

Huddleston's car being driven out of St Peter's Priory, Rosettenville, on
its way to the airport at the time of his departure from South Africa.
Children, staff and brethren of the Community wave goodbye.
Credit:IDAF

Above: A farewell gathering of parishioners at Pimville, which was a large black township built years before and part of parish. *Credit: IDAF*

Left: The first edition of *Naught for Your Comfort*, published in 1956 by Collins. A quarter of a million copies have since been sold, and it is still in print. *Credit: IDAF*

Below: Huddleston with children at St Martin's School, the buildings virtually unchanged since 1956, but with a very different racial composition that promises well for the future. *Credit: Antelope West.*

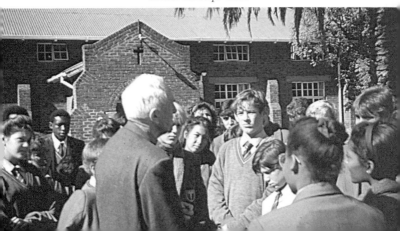

Left: Huddleston with Oliver Tambo in the library of St Martin's. Tambo was educated at the school when it was St Peter's, and taught there until 1953 when he entered a law firm with Nelson Mandela. *Credit: Antelope West.*

Above: A visit to Skeen School, Alexandra Township. Despite having 700 pupils, the school has no running water and little equipment. One class has a single teacher for a hundred children. *Credit: Antelope West.*

Below: A welcome from the headmaster of the Skeen School. *Credit: Antelope West.*

Teenagers on holiday from secondary school, or unemployed.
Credit: Antelope West.

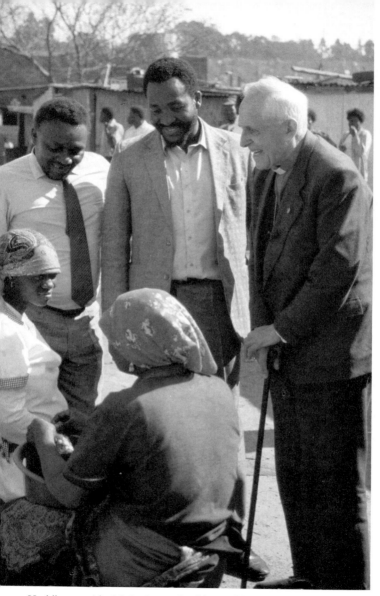

Huddleston with civic leaders and residents of the squatter camp on the edge of Alexandra Township. *Credit: Antelope West.*

Four of the original Huddleston Jazz Band play in the garden of St Peter's Priory, house of the Community of the Resurrection. *Credit: Antelope West.*

Huddleston with Walter Sisulu - sometime prisoner on Robben Island, now Deputy President of the ANC - at Kliptown on the anniversary of the Congress of the People on 26th June 1955. *Credit: Antelope West.*

With old friends (once schoolboys at Sophiatown) at the site of the
Congress of the People. Abdul Minty is on the right. *Credit: Antelope
West*.

Huddleston with Fr Jeremy Platt CR at the squatter camp of Vlakfontein, where he lives and works. *Credit: Antelope* West.

The Huddleston Swimming Bath at Orlando West, Soweto, as it is today 36 years after its opening. It is still in beautiful condition and equipped for international swimming events. *Credit: Antelope West.*

Huddleston gives the opening address at the ANC Conference - the first for 30 years - in the University of Durban, Westville, Natal. There were 2,250 delegates from all over South Africa. *Credit: Antelope West.*

'ecstasy and agony' and thus I cannot address it as if I were not affected by it.

It is clear that Dr Frank Chikane, the General Secretary of SACC, is an outstanding orator. At the age of forty he has also become, with Archbishop Desmond Tutu (a predecessor as General Secretary), one of the greatest Christian activists in the struggle. Oratory is a valuable gift for it enables a leader to move his audience to action. But it can be also a dangerous gift if it does not spring from integrity and has not been the product of TOTAL commitment to truth. That commitment to the truth was, for Frank, the result of a testing which few could have survived unscathed. He was ordained in 1980 and took up a ministry in Krugersdorp strangely enough, the same town in which Desmond Tutu grew up. During this period Frank was arrested several times and in 1985 (at that time President de Klerk was a cabinet minister with seven years in office in the present South African government) he was charged with treason because of his involvement in the United Democratic Front. Released after three months, he went into hiding and then to Europe, but returned to South Africa in 1987 voluntarily and in the same year was appointed Secretary of the SACC. Here is his own account of the torture he endured just six years ago:

> The torture involved being forced to remain in certain contorted positions for many hours until the body gave in. When I could not keep the prescribed positions any longer, I was assaulted with fists and various other objects like a broomstick. At times I was chained against other objects in a crouching position, handcuffed to my feet, and left in that position for a very long time.

49

Once I was hung head down with my hands and feet over a wooden stick, and assaulted in that position. I do not remember much of the details of the latter experience as it looks like I lost consciousness.

Afterwards I was confused, with my whole body completely unstable. Walking was a struggle, and when I arrived at the prison where I was kept, I could not stand steadily as the warders checked me into the prison. I remember the prison warders making a laughing-stock of me, saying I had gone through some good 'music' and that I was continuing to 'dance'. The last ordeal of my six weeks of torture had involved being kept standing in one spot for fifty hours continuously without sleep. I was chained against the bars of the heating system, underfed, interrogated and assaulted continuously by teams of interrogators who changed shifts every eight hours, twenty-four hours around the clock.

It was during this ordeal when I tried to make sense of the Gospel and the sermons I preached about 'loving your enemies'. I began to ask questions about God's power and concern. But one thing that kept me strong and made me survive was the experience of the Lord Jesus Christ; that for the salvation of the world it did not seem like Jesus could have let the cup pass.

The experience of the apostles also kept me strong. For it does not seem as if the Gospel we have today could have been passed over to us without them going through the persecution they suffered even unto death. But as I went through the pain I began to understand that, in fact, Christians have an enormous responsibility in the world, far more than they are aware of. I felt it was a matter of life and death for me to suffer for the sake of others; the weak in our society, the brutalised, for the sake of Christ's body, that is, his Church. I felt more empowered to say to my torturers during my fifty-hour ordeal, men who had told me I was going to die 'slowly but surely', that 'Christ will be honoured in my body whether by life or by death'.

My torturers asked me in the course of this ordeal to make a choice between dying slowly in a painful way and co-operating by collaborating with them against those I am called to minister to. I told them that collaboration and co-operation with the evil racist system in South Africa was out for me. It was a call for me to abandon the very fundamentals of my faith and calling. I told them that instead they had to decide whether to let me die or live, being conscious of the consequences of both options. But I did not have to make the choice; it lay in their hands. Through the pain they made me feel at one stage that if I was to die, then the faster the better.

At one stage they suggested that I should commit suicide to speed up my death. My response was that Frank Chikane did not have the right to take his own life, and, anyway, I was not going to let them off the hook by terminating my own life, and make them feel less guilty after what they had done.

51

By the forty-eighth hour I no longer felt normal enough to be able to continue intelligently answering their questions, and I decided to keep quiet after telling them about my position. I announced that I was not going to answer questions any more. For two hours they tried every method to force me to talk but in vain. On the fiftieth hour I was loosened and driven from Krugersdorp to Rustenburg prison. Throughout my time at Rustenburg I was kept in solitary confinement.

It took me about three months arguing with the magistrates who visited me once in three weeks according to the regulations before I got a copy of the Bible. The security police's argument was that they would not give me a Bible because 'dit maak jou'n terrorist' (it makes you a terrorist). They felt that the Bible did not seem to help me. It is clear that for them, like all oppressive regimes, the Bible helps you only if it makes you submissive to the dictates of the oppressor. When, at last, they did give me a copy of the Bible, they gave me an Afrikaans one, maybe to force me to read their language. But nevertheless it was a blessing to have a Bible, whatever the language.[5]

I have quoted Frank's words verbatim because they speak for themselves of the man's integrity. And, more than any other words I know from within the struggle, they express the ecstasy and the agony of the present moment in South Africa. The ecstasy of February 1990 when Nelson Mandela walked free, with Winnie, from Pollsmoor prison in Cape Town, and thousands there and millions more across the world rejoiced because it seemed certain that a new South Africa had come to birth. The agony, eighteen months later when not only were Natal and Kwa Zulu but towns and squatter camps across the country plunged in violence, the 'peace process' was at a standstill and negotiations between the nationalist government and Mandela had not even started. Nelson had said to me in the car as we drove away from the airport on the day of my arrival, 'The policy of de Klerk and the government is to weaken the ANC and to strengthen the other parties like Inkatha *before* negotiations get under way'. In answer to the question put to him by Lord Hatch as recently as the second week in September this year, 'De Klerk has admitted that his government has funded anti-ANC movements. Do you think he's trying to build an anti-ANC coalition?' Nelson replied, 'Oh, yes, there's no doubt about that. That coincides with some of his statements, that his political and economic policy is closer to that of Inkatha than to that of the ANC. He (de Klerk) made that statement only about a week ago.'[6] The SACC conference was for me the precursor – the premonition if you like – of what I was to experience again and again during my visit: the ecstasy never separated from the agony, Egypt, the land of bondage at last left behind but no Promised Land in sight: only the wilderness.

Yet it is a moment for profound thanksgiving on the part of Christians of all denominations that today it is the Church in its widest definition that is recognized as an instrument of revolutionary change. President Botha told the world that he had 'crossed the Rubicon' – meaning that his government was now committed to creating a new South Africa by a new constitution. He followed that statement by totally excluding the black majority from the tri-cameral legislature he had set up. At the same time the banning order against all political parties remained in place. The media were still under the control of the government. Political prisoners were still in prison. The security forces were given even greater powers by the proclamation of a state of emergency virtually nationwide. And it was only the voice of the Christian Church during the six years that followed President Botha's 'reforms' that could be heard in protest across the world.

Desmond Tutu, now Archbishop of Cape Town; Beyers Naudé, former Moderator of the Southern Transvaal Synod ('the most implacable foe of apartheid that Afrikanerdom has produced'[7]); Alan Boesak, President of the World Alliance of Reformed Churches and founder of the Alliance of Black Reformed Christians; Frank Chikane himself, were, together with thousands of activists within the churches, the voice of the oppressed majority. It was that voice which, when the moment came, and de Klerk succeeded Botha in the Presidency of South Africa, had so strengthened anti-apartheid bodies worldwide that it was clear to the international community beyond doubt that apartheid must be destroyed. In its 16th Special Session on 14th December 1989 the United Nations General Assembly issued a Declaration on South Africa which was adopted by consensus, that is without a single nation dissenting. 'In pursuance of the objectives stated in this Declaration', it reads, 'we hereby decide: To step up all-round support for the opponents of apartheid . . . To use concerted and effective measures, including the full observance by all countries of the mandatory arms embargo, aimed at applying pressure to secure a *speedy end* to apartheid. To ensure that the international community *does not relax existing measures* aimed at encouraging the

54

South African regime to eradicate apartheid *until there is clear evidence of profound and irreversible change* bearing in mind the objectives of this declaration.'

No one would dare to claim, and I would certainly not even wish to, that it was the voice of the Church in South Africa that aroused the international community, through the UN Declaration, to effective action. It was the long, heroic struggle and endurance of the black majority inside South Africa which brought us all to that great moment of decision. But it certainly was the voice of Christian leaders like Tutu, Naudé, Boesak and Chikane that carried the message to the outside world.

Compared with the days when I was in South Africa and when increasingly, and especially through the State's Bantu Education Act, massive repression was enforced by law, the Church's role had changed absolutely. Today it is the Church which identifies itself unreservedly with the liberation movement and which has a leadership prepared to act. These days of transition will certainly put it to the test. I believe it will not fail.

4

With the removal and physical destruction of Sophia-town, the only other comparable black township to survive with its freehold status intact is Alexandra. It has had to fight hard for its survival, but it is recognizably the same place as it was in 1956 – though its population has greatly increased. Although much further away from the centre of Johannesburg than Sophiatown it too was providing the city with a large part of its labour force. Thousands of workers bussed in early each morning and bussed home late in the evening. When the Public Utility Corporation (PUTCO) which owned the buses decided in 1956 to increase fares, the Alexandra citizens organized a bus boycott and, for weeks on end, walked the twelve miles each day to work and back. That boycott was still in force on the day I flew out of Jan Smuts airport on my way to the United States. I carried with me in my thoughts the picture of the Alexandra protest: yet another image of the evil consequences of apartheid because, of course, PUTCO had the absolute monopoly of transport services for the black workers of Alexandra.

In the USA I asked to visit, as soon as possible, the Deep South. With an American lawyer I was taken to Montgomery, Alabama, and advised to meet one of the Baptist ministers of that city. His name was Martin Luther King, and in 1956 he was only beginning to be heard of outside Alabama. He had supported a bus boycott in protest, not at fare increases but at segregation on public transport. Already fire-bombs were being thrown through his windows. He said to me, in describing the situation, 'You know Montgomery was the HQ of the Confederate Army in the Civil War. They call it "The Cradle of the Confederacy". Well – it's sure rockin'.' So we talked of Alexandra and the meaning of protest action against racism and the universality of such action: the need to use non-violent means even if it provoked violent reaction. We certainly spoke a common language in that brief encounter, but I never had the opportunity to meet Martin Luther King again.

On 26th June, South Africa Freedom Day, I returned to Alexandra Township just as its children were pouring into school for the first lesson of the day. It was as if the years between had not existed. I could have been walking across Meyer Street from the Priory surrounded by the same throng of chattering, laughing, noisy kids moving apart to make way for me at the school entrance. I almost began to look for familiar faces so that I could greet them by name. They wore the same simple uniforms I remembered; they had the same 'shining morning face'; the same smile. The primary school chosen for my visit had been built (no doubt as a 'mission school' in those days) in 1943. Although it showed signs of wear and tear it was noticeably clean and tidy. In fact children were still sweeping the corridor outside their classrooms to make sure it was ready for our arrival (Abdul was with me for his first visit to a school since he left for exile). The Headmaster told us that there were some seven hundred pupils, and he opened the door to the classroom of the first grade. There were a hundred children closely packed together. 'They have no desks,' he said, 'they must use their chairs.' Their teacher (only one teacher) said, 'Get up and show how we manage'. It was a swift operation, turning the seat round, kneeling on the floor in front of it and balancing the book ready for action.

In that school of seven hundred children there was no water supply. The teachers were responsible for bringing with them large plastic containers so that, in the break, each child could at least have a cup of water. We went to see the playground. Understandably it was too small for so many children to have enough space if they were all there together. Space in Alexandra is in any case at a premium. Along the side of the playground nearest to the school buildings stood a row of latrines. They were in fact built over buckets and had a trap-door at the back for the removal at night of their contents. The stench was permeating the playground, the buckets overflowing, children unable, in fact, to use them and preferring to use the open space between. The headmaster explained that a new system was to be installed, but he was still waiting. And no water. When we met the teachers in their common room during the break they said, 'What are we to do? There are so few books and so little equipment. Yes. The parents have to pay.' It was true that one teacher for a hundred pupils applied only to the newest and youngest class. But the ratio must have averaged one teacher to forty as far as I could judge.

Under the Bantu Education Act the principle of 'ethnicity' in school was mandatory and had been so for nearly forty years. In this school the language medium was Northern Sotho. In the school next door it might be Zulu, Tswana, Xosa or Southern Sotho. Yet Alexandra, like Sophiatown, is a multi-ethnic community and always has been. Children who live in such a community and play together are therefore deprived of a common language unless they can speak English or Afrikaans. It was this

58

issue and the imposition of Afrikaans on top of ethnicity which led to the Soweto uprising of children in 1976. It was the direct and intended result of the Bantu Education Act which came into force on 1st April 1955. Dr Hendrik Verwoerd, introducing the Act in the Senate, said: 'The school must equip the nation to meet the demands which the economic life of South Africa *will impose upon him* . . . there is no place for the native in European society above the level of certain forms of labour.' Later in the debate Dr Verwoerd said: 'I want to remind Honourable Members that if the native in South Africa today, in any kind of school in existence, is being taught to expect that he will live his adult life under a policy of equal rights, he is making a big mistake.' I wrote in commenting on the Bantu Education Act: 'There can be no question that, of all apartheid legislation during the past eight years of Nationalist rule, this Act is by far the most important and *by far the most deadly in its effect*.' Standing in that school playground the other day, with the children around me singing songs of welcome and farewell, I knew that my prophecy had been fulfilled. The deadly effect of thirty-six years of education for servitude will take decades to erase and billions of pounds to replace. It is not past history. It will be the most important and urgent task of whatever government comes to power when the new constitution and the new parliament are in place.

'Liberation before Education' was the cry of the secondary school children through the most recent years of struggle in the townships. It was a cry of anger. Of anger not just against the government of President Botha when his security forces targeted school children, imposing a kind of military presence in the classrooms to discover and record the names of dissidents. It was anger not just against the physical attacks which drove thousands of them into exile, where thousands still remain. It was anger also against parents who had promised them that if they worked hard at their books (when often enough there were no books) they would see a future of fulfilment. 'The ecstasy and the agony' . . . both there in Alexandra Township on 26th June for me and Abdul – himself a victim of that vicious act. Ecstasy, as always, because of the children and their unchanging trust and the magnanimity of their welcome. Agony because, even at their moment of hope for the future, so many of them will never have the full opportunity to develop and use their talents and skills. The process of change will take too long. And 30% of the child population of Alexandra have not had the chance of education at all.

On the day of our visit there appeared to be a particularly visible military presence. Helicopters overhead, Caspirs – those hideous armoured troop carriers – at the corners of the streets, soldiers and police in evidence all over the township. I wasn't so conceited as to think that my visit could cause such armed vigilance. So what was the reason? I discovered the reason later in the day. A special form of protest had been organized in which children from one school in Alexandra would leave their overcrowded classrooms and unusable latrines and would occupy one of the many white schools closed and empty because there were not enough children to fill them (the white birthrate has fallen considerably in recent years). This school was in the suburb of Orange Grove, Johannesburg, one of the nearest suburbs to Alexandra, and the children were to be bussed that morning to make a peaceful demonstration against such an unjust education system. They were prevented from doing so by armed force.

When I met the Alexandra Civic Association later in the morning I was given the chance of discussing with them the future of their city – for such it truly is. And after our meeting they accompanied me in a tour of the place, so familiar and yet so changed. Grossly overcrowded, yet with adjacent land unoccupied. A squatter camp of hundreds of shacks adjacent to the boundary – yet a well organized group of women working together with an American voluntary agency on a housing project. A small group of teenagers playing dice at a corner of the squatter camp, some in school (it was the vacation) others despondent and jobless.

But the most encouraging development was what the 'Civics' called The Alexandra Accord. After six months of negotiations about the future, the Accord was signed on 27th February 1990 by representatives of the Government (in the form of the Transvaal Provincial Administration), the Alexandra Civic Organization (known as the Civics) and the Alexandra City Council (local government). Its purpose is an agreement to deal with many of the problems facing Alexandra: land, housing and services such as water, sewerage and electricity. The residents will have the opportunity to discuss such issues and put forward suggestions about the future. Meetings will be called in all areas so that there can be full participation by the residents in decisions about the future. But, most important of all, there will be a Joint Negotiating Forum to find the most practical way of solving the problems of Alexandra. By the time we met the 'Civics', the Accord had brought about an end to the long 'rent boycott' and all rent arrears had been written off. It was agreed that there should be special interim prices for services such as water, sewerage and rubbish removal. R3 million was provided by the

Regional Services Council to improve the water system, upgrade the latrines and improve the electricity supply, and an affordable price list for all these things had been negotiated and approved. Only a beginning, but at least a beginning in which fully democratic structures are in place and a truly representative organization has been set up. After so many years of struggle for survival Alexandra is still there. In spite of everything that is so destructive of human dignity, it is a sign of hope.

*   *   *

In the afternoon of the same day as my visit to Alexandra, Walter Sisulu picked me up at our hotel to take Abdul and myself to Kliptown, a place which is now part of the mythology of the struggle because it was the place where the Freedom Charter was proclaimed and agreed clause by clause. The days on which this happened were 25th and 26th June 1955, and the occasion was the Congress of the People. Helen Joseph, that great campaigner against apartheid, described her memories of that gathering thirty-six years ago: 'The idea for a mass gathering of people from all over the country came, I believe, from Professor Matthews of the ANC.' For eighteen months a hard core of volunteers – 'I can't remember how many thousands there were, there were so many' – pledged themselves to find out from the people what their priorities would be in a free South Africa. The concept of a Charter embodying those demands and put to the vote of a fully democratic gathering 'of people in the fields, in the factories, in the streets, in the houses', of every race, colour and creed, was the purpose of the Freedom Charter. It was not a formal gathering, but it was a quite remarkable, indeed unique expression of grass-roots democracy. A co-ordinating committee representing the

Congress movement, the African National Congress, the South African Indian Congress and the Congress of Democrats of the Coloured Peoples Organization raised funds to pay the costs of transport and publicity.

On the day itself some three thousand people began to assemble. In Helen's words, 'Bus after bus, lorry after lorry came up to that large open space like a football field in the middle of the straggling township of Kliptown. They had slept all night in their lorries or buses and many of them had travelled hundreds of miles. With their banners they marched into the enclosure, each banner expressing their demands: "Away with Bantu education . . . We want better houses, We want a living wage, We want the vote". And they marched in to say, "We're here . . ."."

Like Helen I have the most vivid recollection of that day. It was a mixture of a vast election rally and Derby day: full of colour and movement and singing. Yet, at the same time it reflected the single unifying purpose of the whole event: the endorsement of the Freedom Charter. There was the consciousness that this was an historic moment in the struggle and that the two days must not be wasted.

In a deliberately symbolic way three of us were chosen for a special ceremony, the presentation of the Isitwalandwe award – the highest honour that the ANC can bestow. It was to be given to Albert Luthuli, President of the ANC; to Yusuf Dadoo, President of the South African Indian Congress; and to myself, the first white person ever to receive it. But both Luthuli and Dadoo were banned and could neither leave their homes nor attend any gatherings, so in fact I was the only recipient. Originally the feather of a great bird it was, on that day, a simple circular medal of silver with the wheel and four

63

spokes engraved on it: the four spokes symbolized the four races, African, Coloured, Asian and White, of South Africa. The inscription on my own medal simply states, 'To Father Trevor Huddleston for outstanding service in the cause of South Africa's Freedom, 25/6/1955.' It is the most precious honour I have ever received, or ever shall. The wives of Luthuli and Dadoo received their husbands' medals on their behalf.

The Freedom Charter, read out in English, Sesotho and Xhosa, began:

> We, the people of South Africa, declare for all our country and the world to know, that South Africa belongs to all who live in it, black and white, and that no government can justly claim authority unless it is based on the will of all the people; that our people have been robbed of their birthright to land, liberty and peace by a form of government founded on injustice and inequality . . .

Its aims, spelt out in ten long paragraphs, were all concerned with human rights, equality, the fair distribution of land, the just wage, work and security, and opening the door of learning and culture to the whole population. Some of the aims were generalities, but all of them came from the hearts and minds of those who had responded from village and township and city to the single question, 'What kind of South Africa do you want?'

On our drive to Kliptown I had my first view of the vastness of Soweto after my long absence. When I left in 1956 the name Soweto (*So*uth *We*stern *To*wnships) had not been thought of. It was still a conglomerate of municipal locations sprawled across the veldt, row upon row of identical 'matchbox' houses, minimal street lighting if any, and the churches and schools built and maintained by many denominations. Main roads to the townships and linking them were strategically planned to make it easy for military and police vehicles to move swiftly from east to west, north to south, but the streets were made of the sandy soil on which the whole of Soweto is built. A landmark in those days, still dominating the skyline in 1991, were the massive cooling towers for electricity supplies, not for Soweto but for Johannesburg's white suburbs and industrial plants. It was reckoned that in the '50s the population was a million and a half and rising. Today it is between three and four million including the old townships of Pimville and Kliptown and the squatter camps still on the periphery of 'locations' like Orlando, Meadowlands, Jabavu and the rest, all built after I left South Africa in 1956. The vast population increase is matched by what I believe to be the largest hospital complex in the world: Baragwanath Hospital. It started life just a year before I arrived in Sophiatown and its beginnings were in the form of single-storey wards made of timber, linked by covered concrete paths and, presumably, the necessary theatres, casualty and outpatients departments. But in fact it had been built in the first place as a TB hospital for allied troops, some of them officers, who had been serving in the Far East.

Of all the developments that have taken place in the apartheid years, and despite all the destructiveness of the apartheid system itself, Baragwanath Hospital is a superb achievement in the excellence of its services to the black community. And it always has been a centre of excellence in training doctors and nurses by the thousand and in pioneering or improving new treatments. It was hard to believe that this vast spread of buildings on the main road alongside Soweto had its origins less than fifty years ago in those simple cottage-hospital-style wards that I had known and visited. Indeed the hardest task I faced on my return was to recognize the places I used to know so well.

It was quite difficult for Walter Sisulu, even eighteen months after his release from prison and his return home, to be sure of the right road to Kliptown. In fact it was his first visit to the place since the Congress of the People, and it too had changed almost beyond recognition. The great open space where the Congress was held had almost disappeared, built over by a shopping centre which left only a small area for market stalls on the dry, scrubby grass. It was there that we gathered for the BBC cameras to photograph us and for Walter to read out the opening words of the Freedom Charter: 'South Africa belongs to all who live in it . . . Restriction of land ownership on a racial basis shall be ended . . . No one shall be imprisoned, deported or restricted without fair trial . . .'.

He turned to me and said, 'You know, I was here on the day of the Congress. I was banned at the time. But I was actually present on the top of that roof over there! On that roof we were not visible for people to see us easily so that we could have been arrested for attending the gathering, but we were near enough to be part of it . . . we saw the multitude of the people gathered there but we left before the action of the police . . .'. He turned to me, took my 'Isitwalandwe' medal and fastened it on the lapel of my coat: just another moment of the ecstasy of my return. To be with Walter on the same ground on the actual anniversary, and to be surrounded by a small crowd of people, one or two of them who were there also on the day itself, but the majority of them who were not even born.

Mary Benson has described what happened after the whole reading of the Charter, section by section, had been approved with shouts of 'Afrika' and 'Mayibuye':

> On the Sunday afternoon came the sound of tramping feet. Police armed with Sten guns marched towards the seated delegates. A shout went up. The crowd rose, hands raised in the Congress salute, and, as the chairman urged them to keep calm, they burst into singing 'Mayibuye!' to its cheerful tune of 'Clementine'. Special Branch detectives and armed police searched speakers and audience, confiscating every document. Even posters and banners were taken, including two notices from the foodstall 'SOUP WITH MEAT' and 'SOUP WITHOUT MEAT'. It was announced that 'treason' was suspected. The meeting continued in a mood that was almost triumphant. At the end all stood and sang 'Nkosi Sikelel' i Afrika'. As darkness fell and delegates began to disperse, the ANC band played freedom songs.[8]

I must be forgiven for allowing myself to dwell upon those two momentous days at Kliptown in 1955. But in fact they had immense significance for the history of the struggle. As Nelson Mandela said at the time, and has repeated many times since his release from life imprisonment, the Freedom Charter had become the cornerstone of policy not only for the Congress Movement and the ANC and all who were there, but thirty years later when the United Democratic Front was formed to resist the government of President Botha. During my three weeks' stay in South Africa, and most particularly at the ANC Conference in July, the Freedom

Charter was quoted again and again as the document that mattered most. 'Never before', said Mandela, 'has any document or conference been so widely acclaimed and discussed by the democratic movement in South Africa. The Charter is more than a mere list of demands for democratic reforms; it is a revolutionary document precisely because the change it envisages cannot be won without breaking up the economic and political set-up of present South Africa.'

But Kliptown had another consequence which signalled unmistakably the government's determination to end all resistance to apartheid in the country at large. After the Congress, the police made over a thousand raids nationwide. They seized countless documents, among them, naturally, Mandela's writings. Mary Benson writes, 'While Mandela, Sisulu and Tambo were being driven by police to the Fort, Johannesburg's old prison, from all over the country military aircraft were transporting men and women of every race to be incarcerated there. Chief Luthuli, Dr Naicker, Professor Matthews; loyal Congress leaders from the past such as Canon James Calata . . . Ruth First, Transvaal editor of *New Age*, the pro-Congress newspaper; her husband, advocate Joe Slovo . . . Lilian Ngoyi and Helen Joseph'.[9] Apart from the leaders the majority of the 156 accused were drivers, clerks, factory workers, labourers, teachers and housewives, Blacks, Whites, Indians and Coloureds. All were accused of high treason. All, after over four years, were acquitted. But, before the trial began, I had been recalled by my Community to England and because of my vow of obedience, I had no choice but to go.

5

The week before the ANC Conference, which was the sole reason for my visit to South Africa and the only justification for a return which I had vowed never to make until apartheid was dead and buried, was a perfect preparation for the Conference itself. It gave me many opportunities, public and private, of meeting those people that I had so reluctantly and sorrowfully left, and of visiting virtually all the places where I had lived and worked. But nothing could have been more deeply moving for me than finding that friendships made forty-five years ago with children in Sophiatown and Orlando had endured in spite of the separation and loss of contact, and were still as strong as they had been then. The names of these boys and girls who surrounded me in the school playground, in church for meetings of the servers' guild or, often enough, in the Priory garden in Meyer Street, have remained with me through the years – and their nicknames too. 'Chinkie' Modiga, a thin little boy with a specially disarming smile, who often used to take my hand and take cover under my thick black clerical cloak as I walked across to church on a winter evening; 'Pulé' and 'Boyza' (their real names were Samuel and Abel), always ready for a ride in car or truck to anywhere and back; Tom Dire who used to caddy at weekends and in the school holidays for white golfers at the Country Club, and who acquired a golf club or two and some old balls and played the game on that open strip between Sophiatown and Westdene that was called the 'colour-bar'; Sally Maunye, beautiful always but never more so than in her uniform as a Girl Guide and 'Brownie' (called, as I remember 'Sunbeams'?) leader.

And so many more – each so incredibly responsive to the love I had for them and to the relationship which that love created across all barriers of colour, age and status. I have no doubt that, for me, it was my vow of celibacy, depriving me of the possibility of having children of my own, of being the father of a family, which made such love for so many children the most powerful force in my ministry. There is far too much inhibition about the relationship between adults and children in Britain, and, I suppose, there are all kinds of reasons – child abuse, whether physical or sexual, one-parent families, the divorce rate and economic and social deprivation. But listen to the voice of Pulé, now a handsome man of fifty or so, speaking of me to Mischa Scorer, in an interview just after I had arrived back home in Johannesburg. Mischa had asked, 'In what way do you think Father Huddleston was different from other priests that you've met?' And he answered, 'He was different in the sense that you knew he was like a father, and he had love you know, love, love, love. Even if you said "Today I've no time for him", he would actually come to you and gather you all around, all of us, all of us . . . I mean other priests were nice to us but the thing is they didn't have that fatherly love . . . Saying "Father", it meant real Father, you know.' And, similarly, Sally, now a little older than Pulé and mother of several children. Mischa asked her, 'Why is Father Huddleston so important in your life?' She replied at some length, describing her own struggle for education (her father was a domestic servant): 'Father Huddleston is a father to me, not a father in the spiritual sense, to me he's a real father

70

. . . I used to run from the Priory to Ekutuleni, from Ekutuleni to the Priory and I was called "the mission child". I played, I took part in the Nativity play that took place in Sophiatown every Christmas time. I played the part of Mary, the Mother of Christ and we were trained by Father Huddleston, and he used to say to us, in order that the play can succeed we must pray with him . . .'

I quote Pulé and Sally to try to convey what I cannot say in my own words: only in theirs. But when I met them both, and many others of my children, I knew the ecstasy, and for those precious moments the agony was not there. And so it was with so many personal reunions: the reality of a love that does not fade or decay or disappear with the years.

There are other reunions I must describe before I attempt to do full justice to the ANC Conference, for it was those meetings which enabled me to realize that my return to South Africa was truly a kind of miracle, never to be repeated, sufficient in itself. In fact everything that will follow that visit, and especially the ANC Conference itself, is bound to be an anti-climax for me, however effectively and swiftly events move to a peaceful resolution of problems and the creation of a democratic state. That is, I hope, not a sign of egotism or unwarranted self-importance. It is simply that my welcome home was so overwhelmingly generous that I know it cannot happen twice.

'Jiji' Mbere was one of the Sophiatown kids who provided the Church of Christ the King with a permanent youth club and myself with the kind of stimulus I needed to commit myself completely to the struggle against apartheid. The reason? My love for them all, corporately and individually, and my hatred of the evil system which was destroying their lives. And the love and the hatred were complementary. In all the years that have followed my departure from South Africa I can recognize their influence as paramount. Indeed, the Anti-Apartheid Movement, for me, has been the essential means of honouring my commitment to them. And Jiji is a living example of what I hoped for for all of them – fulfilment in his chosen profession, medicine, in spite of (or perhaps because of) all the odds stacked against him.

During my time as Bishop of Stepney, I had a message and then a visit from Dr Mbere. He was doing post-graduate medical studies in gynaecology at Hammersmith Hospital and he had come to see whether I could help him with accommodation. His course would last for two years. And so it came about that we renewed our friendship, begun in Sophiatown when he was a small boy with a very bright mind and high ambition.

On my arrival in Johannesburg I was told that Jiji had arranged a party for as many of the Sophiatown kids as he could muster. It would take place in his own home in Westcliffe Drive: the very road in which stood the Bishop's House – indeed, it turned out to be almost next door. Dr Mbere is now a distinguished consultant in gynaecology and obstetrics, working at Baragwanath Hospital but with a considerable reputation in the wider community of Johannesburg; not a few white patients are referred to him by their own practitioners. On the evening of the party the whole of his large ground-floor sitting room was filled with his chosen guests who were all from Sophiatown. Some brought their wives and children with them – all were middle-aged except for the children. I was placed in an armchair in the middle of the room and for at least two hours I was surrounded by Sophiatown, listening to Sophiatown, responding to

Sophiatown: identifying, some times more swiftly than others, behind the adult faces and voices and gestures, the familiar faces, voices and gestures of the children I had known and loved. That, too, was ecstasy without agony, but almost impossible to describe. It was also the reality of the present moment of transition. Thirty-five years ago such a party would have been totally inconceivable. The only black faces in Westcliffe Drive then were the faces of the domestic servants who worked there in the kitchen as cooks, in the garden and as garden 'boys': at table in white uniforms as waiters. No other black presence was tolerated. Those servants who were resident were not allowed to reside under the same roof as their employers: that would have been a criminal offence under the Group Areas Act and the Population Registration Act. If they were resident, their place was in the quarters, often just a single room, at the bottom of the garden. Or if they were employed in one or other of the large blocks of flats they were accommodated in special quarters on the roof.

On that Wednesday evening of Jiji's party, one of his guests was the editor of a black newspaper who joined in the chatter and probed its assertions and assumptions as good journalists are trained to do. As he was speaking and the guests were listening there came in Hugh Masekela: trumpeter of international fame. At last, after the years of exile, he had returned home and happened to be in Johannesburg during the week of my visit. I have recounted his story in *Naught For Your Comfort*, and there is no need to repeat it here. It was Hugh Masekela, aged thirteen, who gave me the inspiration for the Huddleston Jazz Band when he was at St Peter's School, Rosettenville. I gave him his first trumpet and, of course, other boys demanded instruments too, and a jazz band was the inevitable result. Hugh and the trombonist

73

Jonas Gwangwa followed me to England in the late '50s or early '60s and eventually went to music school in the USA sponsored by Harry Belafonte, that great friend and supporter of black South African artists. Hugh's exile had been a long one, not without all the usual ups and downs of a professional musician's journey to the top. He had always kept in touch with me, and at one great Anti-Apartheid concert before 150,000 people, and again at Nelson Mandela's seventieth birthday concert at Wembley, he was a star performer.

For some reason, and I cannot recall the particular conversation that sparked off his reaction, the journalist intervened with a comment implying that Hugh had *chosen* his exile and had chosen the right moment for his return, whereas others had had to carry the burden and heat of the days of banning, repression and apartheid in all its forms, at home. The journalist managed to imply – perhaps without intending to – that I was somehow implicated as a paternalist figure providing sweets for children but no commitment to revolt. Hugh had not spoken until that moment. He intervened with great passion, moved over to my chair, put his arms around me and said, 'Don't let anyone in this room dare to say anything against Father Huddleston. We will not hear it', and a bit more in the same strain. For me it was another moment of ecstasy, as indeed was the whole evening, and above all the lovely warmth and hospitality provided by Jiji and his wife. My last image of that evening was Jiji's fourteen year old son using his video-recording camera to capture the scene with its participants. For me the contrast between the childhood of father and son there in Westcliffe Drive in 1991 was yet another example of the meaning of hope. Of hope which is already, in spite of the violence, the

74

ambiguities of President de Klerk's policies and of the unnecessary delays in the peace process, a *present* reality. It is that hope, as opposed to facile optimism, which will lead on to the only fulfilment worthy of the name: the total destruction of apartheid.

Another meeting which took place during that week was my visit to the Priory – St Peter's Priory – of the Community of the Resurrection, my own religious order and the only family I have.

When it was decided finally to move out of the old Priory in the southern suburb of Rosettenville and to hand over all our buildings to the non-racial church school, St Martin's, a house was needed which could be large enough for a community of up to ten brethren (there are six at the moment) with room for guests, retreatants and specialist seminars, and, of course, a chapel. We chose a 'working-class' suburb, not so far from Rosettenville, in sight of one or two of the worked-out mine-dumps so typical of Johannesburg's original skyline, but perfectly suited to our needs. It would not be appropriate in this short book to describe the present work and way of life of the brethren. I would only say that it is still linked to the kind of pastoral ministry, theological training, openness to all people of whatever colour or ethnic group they be, as was the case from the beginning of our work in Johannesburg. And, at this present moment, through the commitment of one of the brethren, Brother Jeremy Platt, it has a direct link with the squatter camp of Vlakfontein. One of the best moments of my short visit to the Priory was to go there and to spend an afternoon with Jeremy and to experience over again the meaning of 'identification'. As in Sophiatown, Jeremy and, through him, the Community of the Resurrection, were a part of the living community of Vlakfontein. It was another moment of ecstasy, in the midst of the agony of which squatter camps are the most potent symbol, to see in the children and the old people, the trust and love of their greeting. How dull and respectable and infinitely unexciting does the Church of England, as by law established, appear to me. How refreshing and stimulating and infinitely challenging the church in Vlakfontein, so small in number but so real in its witness to the true meaning of, 'None of them said that anything they had was their own: they had all things common'. Even, no, especially, their poverty.

My last weekend in Soweto itself was the perfect prologue for the ANC Conference about to begin in Durban. It was so largely because I spent a good part of it in Orlando West, that district of Soweto built just before my arrival in 1943. Its church, dedicated to the Holy Cross, was the place of my first sermon on Holy Cross Day, 4th September, and one of the liveliest parishes in the Soweto complex. A new church has replaced the one I knew on the same site, dominating Orlando from its rocky eminence and right in the heart of its people. Amongst those people live Walter Sisulu and his wife Albertina. Now the Deputy President of the ANC, Walter still lives in the same house as he did before the Rivonia Trial, conviction and Robben Island. He is still the same vigorous, energetic and lively person that I knew when, hopelessly immature as I was, I began my ministry there with that first sermon. He told me, 'We are going to welcome you here on Sunday at my house by slaughtering a sheep and I want you to come before, on Saturday, to see the sheep we have chosen!'

To slaughter a sheep in the African tradition is the highest mark of welcome, a kind of ritual or sacramental statement which indeed lies behind the traditional doctrine of sacrifice in many religions – not least the Judaeo-Christian faith itself. So it was for me a great honour, another moment of ecstasy; though standing to be photographed with the sheep and looking into those frightened amber eyes was in itself another matter, the ecstasy of the welcome remained. And when we all gathered for the feast around Walter's table, with his family, children and grandchildren it was most certainly the ecstasy which prevailed. How can I ever adequately express what such moments of my homecoming meant and mean to me? Walter, in his speech of welcome said, 'We have slaughtered a sheep to show our joy at the return to his own family of our son after so many years.' Then, pausing, and with that delightful twinkle in his eye, 'He is not a *Prodigal* son, of course'.

On the way to Walter's house to see and be photographed with the sheep, I stopped to visit the Huddleston Swimming Bath, built thirty-six years ago. Again, I have described the origins of that project in *Naught For Your Comfort*. I had had the feeling that perhaps such a visit was unwise. How could such a large bath (it was an Olympic Games sized pool) have survived thirty-six years of constant use by thousands of Soweto children without damage or vandalism or sheer old age? I had no need for fear. Not only were the bath and its buildings undamaged and unspoilt: they were newly painted and in perfect order. Around them had been laid out a lawn with shade-trees and, today, I was told, major swimming contests, some of them at international level, are regularly held there. I am glad to think that if I am to have any visible memorial after death, it might be that swimming bath: a place of joy and refreshment and, yes, cleansing. Perhaps even a place of ecstasy for the thousands of young Africans who use it. 'Si monumentum requiris, circumspice.' Cathedrals are not the only buildings which speak of hope.

My second Sunday in South Africa after my return was also my first in Soweto. I was invited to preach at St Paul's Church Jabavu. When I left in 1956 Jabavu itself was a site for development but was at that time, as I recollect, one of the many squatter camps around the periphery. The church is perhaps the most striking Anglican church in Soweto and I am told that visitors from overseas who want to experience African worship are often advised to go to St Paul's. But it is also one of the Anglican churches which has become the spiritual home of those who were uprooted from Sophiatown and found themselves able to bring what they loved in the Church of Christ the King to this fine new building in Jabavu. The singing was as enthusiastic and strong, the congregation representative of all ages and, on that Sunday, these was a thrilling joyfulness in the whole service which made my welcome home complete. I had to leave before the Mass was over and explained this to the congregation but, as I moved out, so did they! They crowded round me; presented themselves and challenged me to recognize them, they held me in their arms and laughed with me until I was able to persuade them to let me clamber into the car. That church had a new and splendid community centre with every kind of amenity for social gatherings and adult education, and there was also a nursery school-all brilliantly architected and, again, spick and span and cared for. Father David Nkwe (now a bishop) had been responsible for raising the money for all this, and his wife was in the congregation to welcome me and show me round. In fact the library – a fully equipped reading room – bears my name.

After the great meal at Walter Sisulu's house I went to

the Roman Catholic cathedral of Regina Mundi, often seen on our television screens in England as the church which, in so many of the violent clashes between the security forces and the people of Soweto, had been the place of refuge and, only too often, the funeral parlour for the victims of that violence. Its parish priest, who had been at the airport to welcome me a week before, had arranged a great service for all the churches of Soweto, led by their ministers, to greet, me with speeches. The choir had the deserved reputation of being one of the best in the whole country. The singing was certainly the best and the most enthusiastic I heard anywhere on my visit. I spoke for a few minutes to thank them and in the course of my address mentioned that I had been honoured by Walter Sisulu in the traditional manner. One of the ministers responded by saying: 'When you come home for good we shall slaughter ten thousand sheep in your honour!' And so with the singing of the choir and crowd surging about me as I left the platform, I felt well-prepared for the morrow and my flight to Durban for the conference for which I had returned.

6

The 48th National Conference of the African National Congress, and the first to take place after thirty years as a banned organisation, took place in Durban from 2nd to 6th July 1991.

I would stress the statistics: they are a reminder of the fact that the ANC has been in existence since January 1912; it is the oldest political party in South Africa. But in origin it was not a political party at all. It was a movement, its full title being the South African Native National *Congress*.

In his book *Sol Plaatje*, Brian Willan writes, 'The movement was conceived as an attempt to provide a truly united forum for the representation of African opinion and interests, a response to the coming together of Boer and Briton in the Act of Union (1910), and a reaction to their own exclusion from any effective representation in the new political structure that had been created'.[10] It brought together a number of remarkable men who for the previous ten years had been leaders and had formed their own organisations, like the South African Native Convention and the South African Press Association. Already the Transvaal Native Congress and the Transvaal Political Organisation had become rival organisations. The quality of the leadership is well illustrated by Pixley Semé, a lawyer trained at Columbia University, USA, and Jesus College, Oxford, who had recently returned home. It was he who issued a famous clarion call for unity at the end of 1911, and it was this determination that led directly to the establishment of Congress, 'the first step towards solving the so-called native problem', the first time that 'so many elements representing different tongues and tribes ever attempted to co-operate under one umbrella'.[11] When Semé's resolution was put to a vote, late in the afternoon of 8th January 1912, 'the motion was passed unanimously and met with loud cheers from the delegates who had risen from their seats'.[12] And Brian Willan comments, 'Even at the time they were in no doubt that they had taken a vital step forward in the history of their people – equivalent in significance, as many saw it to the acheivement of the "whites only" Act of Union.'[13]

John Dube, a Zulu, was elected President, Pixley Semé and Thomas Mapikela treasurers, and Sol Plaatje himself General Secretary. Thus, two years before the First World War and five years before the Russian Revolution, the African National Congress was born. So much for those of its opponents who have accused the ANC of being a 'Communist Front' and who still promote this fiction. It is a pity that so little trouble is taken in Western European governments to know the elementary facts of South African history. But it is also dangerous to the whole future of South Africa itself. Recalling the history of the founding of the African National Congress is an essential element in understanding its 48th National Conference in 1991. It is essential to be reminded of the objects of the organisation nearly eighty years ago if we are to understand its objects for today. They were then defined and unanimously agreed as follows:

(a) The promotion of unity and mutual co-operation between the Government and the Abantu races in South Africa.

(b) The maintenance of a central channel of communication between the Government and the aboriginal races in South Africa.

(c) The promotion of the educational, social, economical and political elevation of the native people in South Africa.

(d) The promotion of mutual understanding between the Native Chiefs and the encouragement in them and their people of a spirit of loyalty to the British crown, and all lawfully constituted authorities, and to bring about better understanding between the white and black inhabitants of South Africa.[14]

As Brian Willan comments in his superb biography of Plaatje, 'By no stretch of the imagination could Congress's aims be described as radical . . . (Congress) resolved now to give added weight to their cause by demonstrating that the new organisation did genuinely represent the African people of South Africa as a whole: to make it impossible for South Africa's white rulers to dismiss their claims as they so often did on the grounds that they spoke only for the educated minority.'[15]

As soon as the Great War ended, and for the second time in their short history, Congress decided to ask the British Prime Minister to receive a delegation in Westminster. Nine people, two representatives from each Province and the President were chosen. They had a clear agenda, requesting the imperial government to revise the South African Constitution 'in such a way as to grant enfranchisement of natives throughout the Union' because only in this way could Africans gain 'a voice in the affairs of the country and have full protection so as to check reactionary legislation and unpopular one-sided laws'.[16]

Prime Minister Lloyd George, to the dismay and anger of the Colonial Office, not only received them but was so impressed by their ability that he wrote to General Smuts saying, amongst other things, 'They were sure that some recent Land Act . . . deprived the native population unjustly of its land and tended to reduce them to the position of wanderers in the country of their birth. They said that they had repeatedly been told that they ought to secure their reforms by *constitutional means* at home. But, they asked, what was the use of calling upon them to obey the law . . . in their agitation for betterment and reform, if they were given no adequate *constitutional* means for doing so . . .' Lloyd George concluded, 'The contrast between the case made by these black men and by the deputation headed by General Hertzog (South Africa's Prime Minister at the time) was very striking.'

To all of which General Smuts (at that time Attorney General) replied that Congress was not a representative organisation: the claims of the delegates were 'more specious than true, and largely amount to *suggestio falsi.*' His government was working on what he described as 'improved machinery for voicing the needs and interests of the Natives', and the delegates should in any case have availed themselves of such *constitutional* means as was at their disposal in South Africa before seeking to publicize their case by 'distortion and exaggeration'.

Although it was thirty years since the ANC had been free to hold its annual conference, the agenda had not changed since 1912: the demand for a new constitution; the repeal of the Land Acts; an educational system properly funded and non-racial in its entirety; the promotion of unity by means of a negotiating process between all parties: and, thus, a non-violent solution to the fundamental divisiveness created and sustained by apartheid ideology.

The enemy still remained apartheid itself. The programme for the 48th National Conference proclaimed on every page the message, 'Transfer of Power to the People for a Democratic Future', and it was that message which was the 'golden string' running through every item on the agenda.

The site for the Conference had been carefully chosen and proved to be ideal from every point of view, not least its beauty. The University of Durban-Westville gained its autonomy only in 1984 and immediately progressed from its apartheid origins as an 'Indian' university to an open university 'committed', according to its prospectus, 'to a democratic, non-racial, non-sexist university and society'. Although it is situated at the heart of South Africa's fastest growing urban centre, the Durban Metropolitan Region, its large campus has a glorious position high among the hills on the eastern seaboard of South Africa. Yet within fifteen years the Durban Metropolitan Region will be home and workplace for some six million people (two thirds of the population of London and just under half the predicted population of New York City). Of those six million nearly three million will be under eighteen years old. In 1990 the University had a student population of 7,800 and the proportion of women was 48%, with nine faculties in all the basic subjects.

The sports centre of the university was the meeting place for the conference and could easily accommodate the two thousand two hundred delegates, plus the hundreds of VIPs invited to its opening and closing sessions.

In July 1990 there occurred perhaps the single most important development in the history of the University – the appointment of a Vice Chancellor, Professor Jairam Reddy, whose anti-apartheid record is beyond question: one of those distinguished academics with an international reputation in the scientific field who had been closely involved in the struggle for democracy in South Africa over the years. His welcome to the university was itself remarkable because, for the first time in its history, students, convocation and staff were joined by representatives of the wider community.

The new Vice Chancellor saw his appointment as representing 'both symbolically and concretely a *decisive discontinuity* with the apartheid origin of the University', and he paid tribute directly to 'those many people at the University of Durban-Westville' who had 'sacrificed their careers and endured periods of incarceration', and to others who were 'the victims of subtle and at times overt repression'. Professor Reddy was our host throughout the Conference and played a major role in ensuring that everything worked as smoothly as possible.

If I have stressed the historical and even physical background to the conference I have done so deliberately. It was a quite magnificent feat of planning and organisation by the ANC and those who worked with them, when little more than a year had elapsed since President de Klerk had removed the banning orders and released the political prisoners from Robben Island and Pollsmoor prisons. It was a matter of re-creating over the whole land the grass-roots organisation of an ANC that had endured thirty years of unremitting harassment and assault by the government. The ANC had lost hundreds of its leaders and thousands had been forced into exile. Whilst, in the years after President Botha's so-called reforms, the United Democratic Front had become a massively powerful opposition, the fact that membership of or contact with the ANC was a criminal offence certainly did not lessen the task of mobilisation in towns and villages in every one of the fourteen regions. For the basic requirement of the conference was that delegates should be *democratically* elected. In the same way that the Kliptown Congress of the People, thirty-six years before, drew its strength from the manner in which those who assembled there were fully representative, so it had to be with the ANC Conference of 1991.

Although I had been asked to open the Conference with prayers – a tradition going back to the foundation of the African National Congress itself – it was only two days before the start of proceedings that I was asked to give a ten-minute address. And it was only on the day itself that I realized what a great honour was being conferred on me. Indeed I cannot think what honour could have been greater than to be garlanded with the Black, Green and Gold colours of the ANC and to stand on the platform with Oliver Tambo, Nelson Mandela, Walter Sisulu and the whole National Executive of the ANC. I had joined in the singing of 'Nkosi Sikelel' i Afrika' – 'God Bless Africa' – hundreds of times at rallies and gatherings in London and across the world, when we were campaigning for the Anti-Apartheid Movement or at meetings of the International Defence and Aid Fund. This was the first time I had joined in singing it with those for whom it was written after my thirty-five years of exile. Never had it been more meaningful. The inspiration of seeing a vast audience in front of me was great enough to carry me through the address I had prepared, although I felt so inadequate in my execution of the task. I was to learn from my involvement with the Conference every day the meaning of democracy in action. It was shown by the extraordinary attentiveness of every delegate to the subject matter of each debate. Amplification of the speeches from the platform and from the floor, and simultaneous translation where necessary (though all the business was conducted in English) made for full participation and discussion. The chairmanship, shared out amongst senior members of the Executive like Walter Sisulu and Joe Slovo, was exemplary. And the handling of interventions and points of order from the floor was both patient and disciplined. There was a determination to treat every issue as needing time and an equal determination to be efficient in the use of procedural checks and balances, and to prevent delegates exceeding the necessary limits set by Conference itself on amendments and the like. I concluded my own address with the words of William Blake that I have already quoted:

> I give you the end of a golden string
> Only wind it into a ball
> It will lead you in at Heaven's Gate
> Built in Jerusalem's wall

'the gate of human dignity and Justice and Freedom', I added. I was followed immediately by the presidential address of Oliver Tambo. Fittingly it was devoted to the history of the struggle during the thirty years of his leadership in exile of the organisation. Of necessity it was a long speech and very hard to abbreviate. It is even harder to convey to those who did not hear it the way in which the quality of Oliver Tambo's leadership, its wisdom, its integrity and its steadfastness, shone through every word. I must confine myself to its three concluding paragraphs:

> Operating within the logic of a people's struggle – armed and political, and supported by the international community – we managed to push the enemy into a crisis which could not be resolved within the confines of the old order. For the first time possibilities to end apartheid and national oppression through negotiations were created. As a result of struggle the closed door that our late President, Chief A. J. Luthuli, knocked on for many decades was finally opened. It is our responsibility and destiny to seize this historic opportunity.

> In this regard, it was vital that we did not surrender the initiative to our adversaries. We initiated a process of wide-ranging discussions within the ANC, between the ANC and the Mass Democratic Movement and between the ANC and the OAU and, in particular, the Frontline states. These consultations resulted in the adoption of the Harare Declaration by the OAU in 1989, the endorsement of this declaration by the non-aligned Movement and the Commonwealth and the adoption of the UN Consensus Resolution on South Africa of 1989.

> Once more, the world stood united behind democratic forces in this country. The unfolding democratisation process is, therefore, taking place on the basis of the agenda set by ourselves. Accordingly we must continue to assert the ANC's leadership of this process. This means

that we have an ongoing responsibility to lead the process of negotiations. As in the past, our leadership should be exercised both here and abroad. This becomes even more important given the changing face of the international community. We must, therefore, re-focus international attention on the need of continued support, including support we shall need in order to reconstruct our country and the region in the post-apartheid era.

The keynote address to the Conference, after President Oliver Tambo's moving account of the years between the last Conference and the present gathering, was clearly to be that of the Deputy President, Nelson Mandela. With Walter Sisulu, Ahmed Kathrada, Reg September, Gertrude Shope, Joe Slovo and Jacob Zuma – the Praesidium – behind him, and over two thousand delegates in front, the stage was properly set. The atmosphere was one not of tension, but of total attentiveness: the silence of anticipation and of hope. Again, to report such an atmosphere is virtually impossible and almost equally impossible is it to do justice to the speech itself, so wide-ranging and so carefully prepared. I had heard Nelson speak in the year before his imprisonment. He was never a rabble-rouser nor a demagogue. With his lawyer's training his words were always carefully chosen and all the more effective for that. The most memorable words were those he spoke at the Rivonia Trial in 1962 and no doubt many of the older delegates would be recalling them: 'During my lifetime I have dedicated myself to this struggle of the African people. I have fought against white domination and I have fought against black domination. I have cherished the ideal of a democratic and free society . . . it is an ideal which I hope to live for and achieve. But if need be it is an ideal for which I am prepared to die.' So now, at the age of seventy-two, he rededicated himself to that idea. The best I can hope to do in conveying that rededication is to let his own words speak for themselves by extracting just a few salient passages:

> It will therefore be required of each one of us that we approach all issues on our agenda with all due seriousness. We expect of all of us rational and constructive debate. Out of that debate must come equally rational, constructive and realistic decisions, aimed at taking South Africa forward as quickly as possible to its destination as a united, democratic, non-racial and non-sexist country . . .

> We have with us many of our friends from the rest of the world who, only a short while ago, would not have been able to enter this country. They have come here at the invitation of the ANC in order to demonstrate their continuing solidarity with our cause . . .

> As a result of the struggle that we waged for decades, the balance of forces has changed to such an extent that the ruling National Party, which thought it could maintain the system of white minority domination for ever, has been obliged to accept the fact that it has no strength to sustain the apartheid system and that it must enter into negotiations with the genuine representatives of the people. Negotiations constitute a victory of our struggle and a defeat for the ruling group

which thought it could exercise a monopoly of political power for ever.

When we decided to take up arms, it was because the only other choice was to surrender and submit to slavery. This was not a decision we took lightly. We were always ready, as we are now, to seize any genuine opportunity that might arise to secure the liberation of our people by peaceful means . . .

The point which must be clearly understood is that the struggle is not over, and negotiations themselves are a theatre of struggle, subject to advances and reverses as any other form of struggle . . .

There are therefore some issues that are non-negotiable: among others our demands for one person one vote, a united South Africa, the liberation of women and the protection of fundamental human rights . . .

Therefore it is necessary that we should have an idea of the time-frame we visualise for the processes which must take us to the election of a parliament representative of all the people of our country.

What, then, are the principal steps that we foresee on the road to this goal? First of all, there remains the matter of the complete removal of obstacles to negotiations as spelt out in the Harare Declaration. This must now include the question of the ending of the campaign of terror against the people, in this province, in the Transvaal and in the rest of our country.

When these issues have been attended to, we should then move to convene the all-party congress. Out of that congress must emerge a number of very important decisions. These will include agreed constitutional principles, the mechanism to draw up the new constitution, the establishment of an interim government and the role of the international community during transitional period.

We still have to grapple with the fact that the process of the removal of obstacles to negotiations has not yet been completed. We will discuss this question, bearing in mind both the progress achieved and what still remains to be done. One of the issues we must note carefully is the way in which the government has acted to discredit the process of negotiations, by dragging its feet in terms of implementing what has been agreed.

This has come as no surprise. It has never been on the agenda of the National Party to enter into negotiations with anybody other than those whom it had itself placed in supposed positions of power. It is also in this context that we should understand the use of violence to derail the peace process.

All of us present in this hall know that there are people within our country, and within state structures, who remain opposed to the transformation of our country into a non-racial democracy. Not only do these forces of reaction stand against the realisation of that ultimate goal, they are also opposed to each and every step that has so far been taken to build towards the accomplishment of this objective.

They did not and do not like the fact that agreement was reached to release all political prisoners and detainees, to allow the free return of all exiles, to terminate political trials, to end the state of emergency, to review security legislation, and so on.

The regime took fright at the prospect of these agreements being implemented because they knew that sooner or later this process would lead to the democratisation of political power in our country and, therefore, the creation of the possibility for the people themselves to dismantle the system of apartheid and create a society that would be in keeping with the genuine aspirations of all citizens of our country. That is precisely why there has been the escalation of public violence such as we have experienced during the last twelve months . . .

From all that has happened so far, it seems clear that this period is likely to prove one of the most difficult, complex and challenging in the entire life of our organisation. It is therefore one which we must all approach with the greatest vigilance and firmness with respect to matters of principle, clarity with regard to strategy and timeousness and flexibility with reference to tactical issues . . .

We must also discuss the issue of the mechanism to draw up the new constitution. As all of us know, we are convinced that this mechanism should be an elected constituent assembly, and we have made this into one of our major campaigning slogans . . .

The international community continues to be of vital importance to the future of our country. This will remain the case even after we have won our freedom. In both the Harare and UN Declarations, it is visualised that a stage will be reached when this community will determine that we have arrived at an internationally acceptable solution to the South Africa question. This would then enable the rest of the world to welcome democratic South Africa as an equal partner among the nations of the world . . .

We consider the South African Communist Party a firm and dependable ally in the common struggle to rid our country of the system of white minority rule. We will therefore rebuff all attempts to drive a wedge between our two organisations.

At the same time, the point must be borne in mind that the SACP is a separate organisation which does not seek to dominate the ANC as the ANC. The ANC, for its part, does not seek to dominate the Communist Party. The policies of the ANC are not decided in the Communist Party as neither are the policies of the SACP decided in the ANC, regardless of the number of people who might be members of both organisations . . .

The continued support of the international community remains vital for the victory of our cause. We need further to strengthen our links with the rest of the world to ensure that the international community, so well represented here today, remains engaged not only in the struggle against apartheid but also in the struggle for the democratic transformation of our country.

From this international community we shall therefore require continuing political and material support for the present phase of our struggle. But equally we will need to prepare these friendly nations to come to our aid as we carry out the enormous tasks that will face us during the period of the reconstruction of our country, as well as define the place of a democratic South Africa within that international community. These are matters of critical importance to our people as a whole and will have to be discussed bearing in mind this reality.

So much of Nelson Mandela's speech entered into the daily debates and, subsequently, into resolutions formally agreed, that there is no need to expand on the extracts I have made.

The five Commissions picked up on all of them in one way or another and, having discussed them, returned to the plenary session with their relevant decisions. But a great deal of time, energy and passion was expended on the role of women in the African National Congress and its future. Interestingly, the resolution demanding that a mandatory 30% of the National Executive should be women was defeated on the grounds that to prescribe a percentage was in itself undemocratic and, in effect, a diminishment of the dignity and value of women as in all ways the equal of men. Why should they need the protection of this prescribed percentage? Let them be nominated and elected by ballot like everyone else. (In fact when the voting figures for the National

Executive were announced it was found that 20% of those elected were women.) Of the other main subjects referred to the Commissions, the issues of violence, the negotiating process, and the ANC constitution required a lot of debating time. But so did international relations, the issue of sanctions, and education – in fact all the issues which constitute the challenge of this transitional period. And it is in this sense that the 48th National Conference has made its greatest contribution to the future shape of the new South Africa. It is because the Conference gave back the fundamental right of secret ballot to those who for thirty years had been deprived of the vote, *even within their own organisation*, that it was of such significance. For it prepared the ground for the use of voting rights on the basis of 'one person one vote' in the General Election, which has been promised by the de Klerk regime and which is fundamental to the non-racial, non-sexist democracy of the future.

An independent electoral commission had been appointed to conduct the election for the chief officers and National Executive committee: the Independent Mediation Service of South Africa (IMSSA). The procedure for voting was agreed by Conference and three independent persons were appointed to observe the elections and to satisfy themselves that the elections were conducted in a fair manner. They were the Vice Chancellor of the University of Durban-Westville; a former Chief Minister of Kangwane, now a business consultant; and a distinguished States' Counsel and National Director of the Legal Resources Centre. With all these safeguards the elections were 'free and fair', and took a whole day to complete.

One voter, I was told, entered the polling booth of his choice and had not emerged after half an hour. After an hour had passed a member of the commission got anxious. After two hours he entered the booth and asked the voter why he was taking so long to choose his fifty candidates. 'Ah!' he replied, 'I was enjoying myself *so* much.' After thirty years without a vote, the franchise can be paradise. It is time the Western democracies understood a little better than they attempt to do, that their refusal to act effectively against the white minority regime of South Africa since the Act of Union in 1910 has in fact itself been a denial of their own supposed democratic values. It was Great Britain, the colonial power, which deprived the citizens of the Cape Colony of their vote in 1910.

The resolutions adopted by the Conference were all of the first importance since they provided a mandate to the ANC National Executive for its strategy in the critical period of transition. The whole purpose of this book is to give an accurate account of the ANC's position, free from distortion by the media and misinterpretation by political leaders within the international community. In Great Britain during the past thirteen years the stance of the Conservative government has been, as indeed it always was in the days of Empire, a recognition of the South African minority regime as the sole representative of all the people of South Africa. Since, until early in 1991 and the repeal of the Land Acts and the Population Registration Act, the authority of the Pretoria government was entirely based on the principle of excluding five-sixths of the population from land ownership and the franchise, to accept white supremacy in this way was in fact to condone apartheid itself. 'South Africa' meant, and still means to the present government of Great Britain and Northern Ireland, President de Klerk's regime and nothing else. In his speech to the Conservative Party Conference on 10th October 1991, the Foreign Secretary Douglas Hurd devoted only one paragraph to African affairs. He chose to focus on the imminent Commonwealth Summit in Harare and said this: 'On Monday (14th October) the Prime Minister will be flying to the Commonwealth Summit in Harare . . . It is time the Commonwealth made a fresh start. It has spent too long *sticking pins into South Africa*, regardless of what was happening in that country. No wonder so many people have forgotten that the Commonwealth is formidable *when it is properly focused* . . .' He then went on to call upon the Commonwealth to 'help some of the members towards good government', free elections, an independent judiciary, a free press, an end to corruption. The 'pin-sticking' to which he was referring was the imposition of sanctions on the South African regime by all Commonwealth summit conferences for the past fifteen years. It was Great Britain alone which, at summit meetings of the Commonwealth, consistently opposed the imposition of economic sanctions on South Africa and most reluctantly joined the consensus on one or two measures which might improve its standing in the international community.

In its resolution on the foreign policy of the ANC, the Conference reaffirmed the Freedom Charter as 'the basic policy document of the ANC', resolving as follows:

> Aware that our foreign policy must be informed by the understanding that South Africa has entered a critical period in the struggle to end the apartheid system and establish a non-racial and non-sexist democracy, and that the white minority regime has been obliged to accept the demand for genuine negotiations, as outlined in the Harare and UN Declarations, which, among others, envisage the following strategic stages:
>
> a) the removal of obstacles to negotiations;

b) the acceptance of interim mechanisms to oversee the period of transition from apartheid to a new democratic order;

c) the adoption of a democratic constitution, the democratic election of a representative parliament and the establishment of a new government;

Also aware that the victories scored by the democratic forces, including the fact that the regime has been obliged to repeal the so-called legislative pillars of apartheid, have given rise to a tendency among a growing number of countries towards the premature lifting of sanctions against the apartheid regime as a reward for the measures undertaken by the de Klerk regime;

Cognisant of the fact that ways and means should be found by which to arrest the process of the erosion of sanctions to ensure that the democratic movement does not lose this weapon, which will be required until a democratic constitution has been adopted;

Reaffirming that the main thrust of our foreign policy must be the attainment of the objectives contained in the Harare and UN Declarations, namely, mobilising the world community to assist towards the speedy eradication of apartheid as well as helping to move the process of negotiations forward towards the creation of a non-racial and non-sexist democratic South Africa;

On sanctions: The primary objective of sanctions is to end apartheid. Since, despite the measures which the regime has been compelled to take, apartheid is still in place, the international community must continue to utilize this weapon to maintain pressure on the regime to expedite forward movement to the attainment of the objective of a non-racial democracy;

Because it is essential that the sanctions weapon is not lost, the international community should be urged to listen to the view of the democratic forces and not seek to reward the apartheid regime. Sanctions must therefore be used creatively in order to arrest the erosion that has occurred, push the peace process forward and attain the objective of a democratic South Africa as speedily as possible.

Accordingly, sanctions should continue to be used as a necessary form of pressure, specified groups of sanctions should be used to achieve the strategic objectives listed below, each one of which is critical to the process of transformation:

a) the removal by the regime of obstacles to negotiations as stipulated in the Harare and UN Declarations, as well as the implementations of effective measures by Pretoria to end violence;

b) the installation of an interim government according to agreed transitional arrangements and modalities on the transition to a democratic order;

c) the adoption of a democratic constitution and

the holding of free and fair elections for a non-racial parliament and a representative government.

In this connection, the National Executive Committee, as a matter of urgency, is called upon, in consultation with our allies, to determine the precise formulation of this process, acting in broad consultation internally and in co-ordination with the anti-apartheid forces worldwide. These forces include the OAU, the UN as well as non-governmental anti-apartheid and solidarity forces.

On the mobilisation of anti-apartheid forces: the Anti-Apartheid Movement worldwide has greatly assisted in creating an extensive world constituency that has compelled governments to place the issue of apartheid on their political agendas. This constituency has also served as an important source of material assistance.

It will easily be recognized that in this comprehensive resolution on foreign policy the issue of sanctions is addressed in a positive and responsible manner. Here is an appeal to the international community, not just to the Commonwealth but to the United Nations, the Organisation of African Unity, the EEC and the USA, to sustain its pressure on President de Klerk's regime until 'fundamental and irreversible change' has been achieved. Until, that is, the repeal of all apartheid laws is completed by a new constitution, free and fair elections and an *interim government* leading to an elective assembly/parliament on a non-racial foundation.

'Sanctions' is not, and never has been, an end in itself.

Sanctions can and should end as swiftly as possible. But not before apartheid is dead and buried.

The final declaration, published by Conference on 6th July 1991, stated: 'The possibility of eradicating apartheid by peaceful means has emerged through our struggle. The overwhelming majority of South Africans are convinced that the process of peaceful transition to a democratic future must proceed with all deliberate speed.'

The only day-long session of the Conference at which I was not present was that on Thursday 4th July, when I journeyed to Pietermaritzburg to visit that area in South Africa which had been, and still remained, the focus of violence.

In its adopted resolution on this subject Conference was to state:

> Many thousands of our people have been attacked and killed, and continue to be killed, especially in the recent period by apartheid-sponsored violence carried out by Inkatha, Askaris, Bantustan death forces and others whose aim is to weaken and destroy the ANC and other democratic forces.
>
> This violence is taking place in a counter-revolutionary context directed by agencies of the state and its surrogate forces in the form of councillors, warlords, vigilantes, death squads and certain white right wing elements.
>
> The ANC, together with other democratic forces such as COSATU, UDF and churches, has attempted to find peaceful solutions to violence by:
>
> a) entering into peace talks with Inkatha;

b) making submissions, representations and demands to the South African government to end the violence.

Despite the past peace initiatives with Inkatha, violence still persists, and despite the machinery at the disposal of the regime, it is refusing to take the necessary steps to end the violence.

The response of the democratic forces in dealing with this counter-revolutionary violence has not been adequate, and the December 1990 National Consultative Conference took a resolution to build defence committees and the organisation has made insufficient progress in the setting up of defence committees.

The recent peace initiative by church and business leaders is aimed at involving all organisations in South Africa in strategies to end the violence . . .

We therefore resolve:

1 To support the current peace initiative of the church and business leaders in: a) developing a code of conduct for the security forces b) developing a code of conduct for political organisations c) developing an enforcement mechanism to monitor the codes that will involve a wide range of groupings d) developing a programme of reconstruction.

2 To mandate the incoming NEC to give a deadline to the appropriate structures by which time it must have completed its task of forming self defence units in all areas, and to take definite

steps to provide all possible resources and assistance required.

3 To embark on a programme of national and international mass action within the context of our demands for: a) the removal of all obstacles to creating a climate for negotiations b) the dismantling of all apartheid structures c) an interim government and a constituent assembly.

7

I had known 'Maritzburg well during my time in South Africa from 1943 onwards. I used to visit a community of Anglican nuns who had been in charge of educational work and, with their branch house in Durban, of pastoral and social work as well. In those days it was 'Sleepy Hollow', a small town dominated by the statue of Queen Victoria which defined both its quintessential Englishness and its continuing aloofness from the political turbulence of the Transvaal. But it had a strong academic presence too, in the form of the University of Natal.

Today it is at the very heart of the violence sweeping across the country: more particularly the conflict between Chief Buthelezi's Inkatha movement and the African National Congress. Over four thousand fatalities have been caused by this terrible conflict in the 'killing fields' of Kwa Zulu and Natal itself.

I was welcomed first by the representative of the Centre for Adult Education at the University and then by the Bishop of Natal at a lunch in the Cathedral precinct and afterwards at a multi-denominational service in the Cathedral. Again, although Pietermaritzburg had hardly changed over the intervening years and Queen Victoria's statue still stood serenely undisturbed outside the City Hall, the Cathedral was a new and splendidly designed building, obviously much used by the whole community.

How, then, had such a peaceful part of the country become the most violent? How did it all start? Where will it end? Fortunately for John Aitchison, the chronicler of the struggle (I refer to its wider connotation – the struggle against 'apartheid' and for democracy-) who accompanied me on my tour of some of the worst areas of slaughter, he is himself a qualified historian and is recognisably an objective and competent commentator. I shall use his words (from the 'Unrest Monitoring Project' of April 1991 and others of his documents) to summarize as clearly as possible the answers to the questions I have just posed:

What is the origin and dynamic of the conflict?

'Who fired the first shot is a great preoccupation of historians of war. In the case of the Natal violence it could involve one in a process of endless regression. Was it the murder of four COSATU members in Mpophomeni by Inkatha in December 1986? Was it the coercion by consumer boycott supporters prior to that? Was it Inkatha supporters in Imbali township who chased out radical youth? Was it some youth who threw a petrol bomb at a town councillor's house?

But everybody in the Pietermaritzburg region knows when the big war started. It started in September 1987 when forced recruitment was resisted by young comrades and residents who, though perhaps not particularly attracted to either Inkatha or the UDF, decided they had had enough and resisted.

My analysis of the data from the Natal Midlands

106

(Aitchison 1988, 1989) leads to the following conclusions:

1 a political dynamic to the conflict, particularly in its inception, is present;
2 that urban township strife has spread outward into peri-urban and semi-rural areas and that even the most conservative tribally controlled territory is not exempt from turmoil;
3 the violence seems to have a strong connection to Inkatha's attempt to maintain (or increase) its influence in the region;
4 political violence is becoming embedded into the social fabric.

The evidence from the Pietermaritzburg area shows that the violence during 1987 started in an urban township and therefore is likely to have been of a political nature rather than the result of floods or unemployment and starvation on the margins of the region.

That the violence flowed outwards from the townships adjacent to Pietermaritzburg, engorging itself with deaths as it did, is backed up by the testimony of eyewitnesses such as Tim Smith S J (Smith 1988), who stated of that part of Vulindlela farthest away from Pietermartizburg that, 'up until September of 1987 it was one of the most peaceful places to be. Incidents of violence there were, but isolated and certainly never politically motivated. I remember discussing with some of our men, at a time when violence was rocking Edendale, how we reckoned that it would never reach our area, since our people were too much tied to tradition, and the rule of the chiefs was so strong. Inkatha had ruled unchallenged for years, and although much of its support was lukewarm, there was no challenge to it. How wrong we were. The September floods were the turning point. While we were still assessing the damage, we started to hear of the explosion of violence lower down, in areas like Sweetwaters and Imbubu, and then suddenly it was upon us too.'

This says something about the ripeness for conflict that existed in peri-urban and rural areas of Natal and which everybody seems to have underestimated. It undoubtedly has much to do with the influx of people thrown off white farms, pressure to seek work in urban areas, the battle for land and fuel and the decay and corruption of the traditional system of tribal leadership . . .

In whose interest is the continuation of the conflict?

It seems to me an inescapable conclusion that the continuation of the conflict is not in the interests of the UDF or the ANC or for anybody espousing a democratic, non-racial, unitary state position.

It is not in the interests of COSATU.

It is not actually in the interests of Inkatha, for apart from destroying the very basis of its *realpolitic* moderacy – its non-violence and associated willingness to enter into acceptable compromises with the existing white order, particularly in the economic sphere – it is fast losing international credibility and has fashioned for itself a long-term burden of revengeful hatred for itself in Natal. It makes its chances of governing Natal in some compromise settlement fraught with dangers. Worst of all, the conflict makes it increasingly dependent on the South African state regime.

It is not in the interests of the people Inkatha represents, particularly in rural areas, for whom the conflict has been regressive and destructive in the extreme.

By contrast, it can be seen to be in the (short-term) interest of the South African government for the following reasons:

— It is cheap. The state has not poured material resources into Natal to 'mop up the oil-spots' as it has done in other troubled localities.

— It keeps Inkatha (and hence also kwaZulu) occupied so that it doesn't have the time or energy to address the long-term cost-benefits of its current relationship to the South African state.

— It keeps pressure off the state. It was a great accomplishment that comrades in Natal saw Inkatha as 'the enemy' rather than the apartheid government.

The South African government has built up a fairly formidable body of expertise in setting up and co-opting traditional elements in collapsing tribal societies. It has had decades of experience with bantustan systems which have led to remarkable stability. It has growing experience with destabilisation, often of a violent kind.

In these terms the Natal Midlands conflict could be seen as one of apartheid society's greatest achievements.

Obviously both Inkatha and UDF supporters have mustered arguments as to the origins and course of the conflict. Both sides accept in varying degrees that the root of the conflict is the result of the exploitation and oppression of apartheid that denied political rights and impoverished the black community. In seeking solutions, both political and material needs will need to be met. Genuine, effective, impartial policing is a must. Real opportunities to express political allegiances through non-lethal forms (such as the vote) at national, provincial and municipal levels of government must be introduced. The 'white' city of Pietermaritzburg needs to recognize that the metropolitan area of Pietermaritzburg is one unit and the more impoverished and underdeveloped sections of it have a right to call on the resources of the whole. Economic resources that will lead to full employment are also an urgent necessity. Last but not least, all the moral and spiritual resources of society will be needed to heal the wounds of a conflict that has torn Natal apart. It is a conflict that, if allowed to continue, may well tear South Africa apart . . .

How would you characterize the groupings in this conflict?

There are more groupings than simply Inkatha and the UDF/ANC/COSATU. Key actors include the State and its police, and the KwaZulu Administration and its police. Many of the combatants on the ground are not necessarily clearly aligned to either Inkatha or its political opponents.

Generally Inkatha has represented a more conservative, more tribal, less urbanised, less well educated group. It is almost impossible to distinguish Inkatha from many elements in the tribal and KwaZulu administration. Many of its combatants in the conflict are easily identified senior leaders in Inkatha. Good examples are David Ntombela, the late Chief Shayabantu Zondi and Thomas Shabalala. Combatant leadership is heavily armed and, in the perception of their opponents, almost immune to prosecution. Inkatha is adept at large scale mobilisations backed by coercion, particularly of rural tribesmen and schoolchildren.

The ANC/UDF group is radical (though often in a very unsophisticated way), keen on a more modern way of life, and relatively better educated. It is generally a much younger grouping (though Inkatha's support among rural youth must not be underestimated). Enormous numbers of schoolchildren, unemployed school leavers and school dropouts enable the ANC/UDF group to stage impressive rallies. The group is relatively poorly armed because state action is taken against them. Combatant leadership is largely anonymous and at a very local level. There is no real equivalent of the Inkatha 'warlord'. The people COSATU represents are a more mature and stable element within the ANC/UDF/COSATU alliance . . .

To what extent is the violence on the Reef an extension of what is happening in Natal?

Whether the violence on the Reef is an export (of a para-military type) from Natal will have to be tested in the courts. It may or may not be.

What is clear is that similar dynamics operate there. There are contending political groups (the dominant ANC and now Inkatha trying to make an impression on the national scene), local situations of potential conflict (in group township people versus outsider hostel migrant workers fed up with being harassed by criminal gangs and political youth from the townships), and right wing elements happy to exploit the situation and destroy the movement towards a New South Africa.

What is also clear is that once violence started, the security services were singularly inept at stopping the violence and there is abundant evidence that, as in Natal, police often let armed Inkatha groups mobilize and attack people without doing anything to stop them.

On the day that I visited the Valley of a Thousand Hills – what could be called Alan Paton country – the whole vast view, bathed in sunlight under the blue sky with its scudding white clouds, was beautiful beyond words. Yet it was here, on the very hill where I was standing, that 'The Seven Days War' took place between 25th and 31st March 1990. I listened to an account of it from a woman pointing across the valley. 'They came from there . . . down that hill . . . you see the house in the valley? It is destroyed . . . the people all fled . . . I think I did not eat for seven days . . . Always I had to organize bandages for the wounded . . .' And so her story went on. Words are useless to convey the sense of outrage and of horror: the senseless violence. Never, as the media like to say 'inter-tribal', because there is only one tribe in Natal and Kwa-Zulu: the Zulu nation.

'Statistics are one-dimensional', writes John Aitchison in one of his reports. 'The place where a multi-dimensional meaning is extracted by participants is in the funerals of the victims and in the poetry that has poured out of the conflict and which . . . has given a real insight into the heart of a stricken people.' I quote from a poem by Ellington Ngunezi of Edendale, published in the *Natal Witness* on 15th September 1988:

Death on My Doorsteps

> After seeing their targets
> On the road
> They alighted from a bus
> And gave them chase;
> Then they saw you standing in your home yard
> As their targets ran past the gate,
> They thought you were one of them,
> Gave you chase,
> They caught you, then killed you
> O Lins, Lins,
> A few minutes later
> You laid on the street
> Serene in rivulets of blood.
> I know you've met Mdayisi,
> Tana, S'fiso, Mlu, Magugu, Hleke, Nhlanhla,
> And the rest;
> I am sure you have revised

Your respective brutal deaths.
And there is no complaining
About anything anymore.
And there are no temptations anymore.
And there is no eating, nor smoking,
No drinking, no cinemas,
And there is no womanising
O Lins, Lins
Your movement to heaven
Was a reminder that we are
Not for this world,
We all have to be covered with
Our last blankets some day;
Soil.
O Lins, Lins,
You have reached a stage
Of total tranquillity and eternity.

Violence in South Africa is often linked with the violence, described as 'black-on-black' or 'inter-tribal' violence which has occurred in many African countries since the wind of change blew and independence was achieved from the colonial power.

There is in fact a fundamental difference. The violence in South Africa is directly due to the apartheid ideology which successive governments have imposed by massive force on the black majority population. Of course it has been linked with the colonial or imperial policies of countries which, since the Congress of Berlin in 1884, divided the continent between themselves regardless of ethnic and tribal boundaries. The Belgians, the Germans, the Portuguese, the French and the British therefore set up various systems of domination and carried them through until the end of the Second World War, when the beginning of the Cold War created a new situation. *But not for South Africa.* When the Nationalists came to power in 1948 they coined the word 'apartheid' to describe their ideology and proceeded to impose it by law at every level of life. Between 1948 and 1956 the policy of 'Grand Apartheid' – Dr Verwoerd's strategy – was implemented by amending and strengthening all legislation social, cultural, and criminal, but above all, economic affecting the lives of the majority from the cradle to the grave. This strategy was essentially *violent*. It was structured on the simple principle of state power. And that power was itself based on an even simpler principle: 'shoot first and ask questions afterwards'. The instruments of this power were the security forces, police and military, together with the intelligence agencies, increasingly subsidized by the state for both national and international surveillance.

The results of this increasing suppression of human rights were seen in an increasing awareness by its victims of the necessity to resist apartheid itself. The massacre at Sharpeville in 1960; the school uprising in Soweto in 1976; the final, nationwide upheaval when President Botha announced his 'reforms' to the world and set up a tri-cameral legislature from which the black majority were totally excluded; all of these were the direct result of apartheid itself. The violence which now directly threatens the peace movement and has so greatly hindered the preparation for a negotiated settlement is the most urgent challenge confronting the leadership of the country today.

In the months before I arrived in South Africa, and during my short visit, a great deal was being done to try to meet this challenge constructively. Initiatives had been taken specifically by the churches – through the SACC and by the business community. It was recognized that peace-making and peace-keeping needed realism as well as idealism: that the Groote Schuur and Pretoria agreements were not working because there had been no effective monitoring machinery to enforce them. The ANC Conference adopted a resolution 'To support the current peace initiative of the Church and business leaders, by developing a code of conduct for the security forces and political organisations' and 'an enforcement mechanism to monitor the codes'.

It was as a result of this resolution that 'The National Peace Accord' was accepted by the ANC. It is a lengthy, detailed and comprehensive document of thirty-two pages, 'to signify our common purpose to bring an end to political violence in our country and to set out the codes of conduct, procedures and mechanisms to achieve this goal.' On 23rd August 1991 this Accord was signed by President de Klerk on behalf of the Government, Nelson Mandela on behalf of the ANC and Chief Gatshe Buthulezi on behalf of the Inkatha Freedom Movement. In addition it was signed by some twenty organisations representing a wide range of groupings, religious and secular, across the country. All who signed it stated, 'We . . . solemnly bind ourselves to this accord and shall ensure as far as possible that all our members and supporters will comply with the provisions of this accord and will respect its underlying rights and values and we, the Government signatories, undertake to pursue the objectives of this Accord and seek to give effect to its provisions by way of the legislative, executive and budgeting procedures to which we have access.'

I have no doubt that this Peace Accord is the firmest guarantee possible for the ending of violence and the beginning, however belated, of the negotiating process. It will have the same status, when history comes to be written, as the Freedom Charter itself. And yet (as we have already seen) there are still those committed to preventing a peaceful solution to South Africa's conflicts, who will continue to destabilize negotiation by deliberate and murderous attacks on innocent people.

*　　*　　*

Before the Conference ended I had another duty to perform: a personal visit to the home of Albert Luthuli at Groutville to lay a wreath on his grave and to meet his widow Nokukhanya and other members of his family. Although she is deaf, Mrs Luthuli said in a letter to me after my visit, 'I am blessed with a very sharp eyesight' which, at the age of eighty-nine, is no small achievement. She does not wear glasses. Since 1970 a large number of the family had been in exile in various parts of the world and were only now beginning to return home. 'I am in Congress', wrote Albert Luthuli in 1962, 'precisely because I am a Christian. My Christian belief about society must find expression here and now, and Congress is the spearhead of the struggle.'[17] I can nowhere find a clearer expression of my own position with regard to the ANC.

Luthuli's grave is under a great tree in the cemetery of the Lutheran church just behind his house. It is, as I expected it would be, a simple house, unchanged since his death, but it has become a place of pilgrimage for many people who recognize him as an historic figure in the fight against apartheid. His commitment, like that of Desmond Tutu his fellow Nobel Peace Prize-winner, was based absolutely on his religious conviction that apartheid had to be destroyed because it was evil. Specifically, Abdul Minty and I went to discuss with his widow, daughter and son the possibility of establishing a Luthuli

Peace Foundation before it was too late to recover his correspondence, scattered as it is across the world. In this project we had the full support and co-operation of Professor Jairam Reddy of Durban-Westville University. Consultations have begun between Professor Reddy and a number of relevant groupings around the establishment of an Institute for Peace and Development within the University of Durban-Westville. One element in this project would be the development of community-based programmes around the work of Mohandas Gandhi and Chief Albert Luthuli. Discussions are already under way with the respective families of Gandhi and Luthuli in order to work out ways in which the University could help, in the restoration of their homes, the creation of community-based resource centres and museums, and in developing programmes which continue the work of these two great leaders of the liberation movement.

Certainly there was no lack of visitors on the day I was Mrs Luthuli's guest. We sat outside the house in the morning sunshine, holding hands and drinking cups of tea and answering the questions of the journalists and pilgrims. For me, once again, it was a moment of ecstasy, untinged by agony. To have had, after so many years, that direct link with Albert Luthuli: to find in his widow, daughter and grand-daughter the same commitment that had inspired him; to be in his own house – this alone would have been a sufficient reward for my return to South Africa. I can only hope that the response to our appeal for the Luthuli Peace Foundation will be generous and immediate.

It is vitally necessary to understand the influence of Mahatma Gandhi himself on the development of non-violent opposition to white racism which he learnt in South Africa. In *Gandhi and Charlie*, the story of the friendship between Gandhi and C. F. Andrews, there is a moving description of the incident which effectively changed the history of two continents:

> He (Gandhi) had gone out to South Africa on a business visit to act as a lawyer in an important trial, wherein two Indian merchants were engaged in litigation. Hitherto, he had only a distant knowledge of the colour-bar and had never considered what it might mean to himself if he was personally attacked and insulted. But as he journeyed from Durban and reached Maritzburg this dreadful experience came to him suddenly in its cruel nakedness. He was thrown out of his compartment by the railway official, though he carried a first-class ticket; and the mail train went on without him. It was late at night and he was in an utterly strange railway station, knowing no one. There all night long as he sat shivering with cold, after enduring this insult, he wrestled with himself, whether to take the next steamer back to India, or to go through to the bitter end, suffering what his own people had to suffer. Before the morning the light came to his soul. He determined by God's grace to play the man . . . This was the turning point from which his new life would begin . . . The new life for Gandhi was one of identification with the oppressed among his own people. He organized and led the struggle of the small Indian community (then only 3% of the population of South Africa) against the discrimination of all kinds.[18]

Gandhi's first step was the foundation of the Natal Indian Congress, and in 1904 he and his family founded the ashram at Phoenix Natal as a place where he and his followers learnt the spiritual discipline they needed. Three years later, in 1907, Gandhi began his 'satyagraha' ('truth-force') campaigns first against the pass-laws which required the registration of all Indians in South Africa, and subsequently against a poll-tax which had the effect of binding Indian indentured labourers to unending servitude on the sugar plantations.

It is impossible to exaggerate the influence of Gandhi on the leadership of the struggle in South Africa, pre-eminently the philosophy of non-violence which was taken into the very heart of the South African Congress movement. Indeed it was Gandhi, not Karl Marx or Lenin, who really inspired Sol Plaatje and his compan-ions, even perhaps without their knowing it, to launch the South African Native National Congress on a basis of non-violence. Even when the Native Land Act of 1913 was passed, and throughout the long years till the Sharpeville massacre of 1960, that principle was dominant. Albert Luthuli was certainly Gandhian in that respect. His Nobel Peace Prize was a recognition of his dedication to what he believed to be the way forward to liberation for his own people. And so the time has come for the kind of development envisaged by Professor Reddy, for the work of Gandhi and Luthuli to be given shape and form in perhaps three ways: first, to make sure that the Luthuli family home is preserved in its present form, with his pictures, furnishings and books as he left them, but to be a permanent museum or memorial to him in much the same way as the house of Indira Gandhi in New Delhi is preserved. Obviously a new home for Mrs Luthuli and her children would need to be built in the grounds of the original house and the family should be relieved of the burden of welcoming and giving hospitality to the visiting public. Second, the actual archive of letters, speeches and all other communications should be given a permanent home, possibly at the Gandhi Centre at the University of Durban-Westville, possibly at Groutville. And third, there should be a living memorial in terms of Albert Luthuli awards and bursaries, to continue the necessary research into the peaceful resolution of conflict: to study in depth the instrument of sanctions as a means to this end, and to keep the conscience of the world alive to and aware of Albert Luthuli's contribution to the peace process in South Africa.

The final day of the Conference ended, as I have said, with the closing address of Comrade Nelson Mandela, now elected President of the African National Congress. So full of debate had that final day proved to be that it was in the early hours of Sunday morning that it drew to a close. A group of political prisoners, just released from prison, arrived just in time for that closing address and received a heroes' welcome.

A rally in the National Stadium took place that afternoon and the vast crowd greeted the newly-elected National Committee, led by Oliver Tambo its Chairman. Appropriately it was slightly delayed by heavy rain. 'Appropriately', because rain in Africa is the symbol of blessing, and we sang and raised our arms in salute for the last singing of 'Nkosi Sikelel' i Afrika' – God Bless Africa.

8

On the following morning Abdul and I flew down to Cape Town. Greatly to my surprise (because my years in South Africa were spent in Johannesburg and the Transvaal), there was a splendid welcome awaiting my arrival at the airport. The ecstasy of that welcome was provided for me by a choir of schoolchildren singing the songs of freedom with their usual enthusiasm. There were old friends, white as well as black and coloured and Asian. It was sheer joy, until a message was brought to me saying that Michael Mapangwana, leader of the Civic Association at Kwaelitsha squatter camp, had been murdered. He had been trying to mediate in a long-standing dispute between rival taxi firms (taxis are not taxis as we know them, but small buses, essential to transport the labour force to and from work, and highly politicized). That was the agony which met me so often as I moved around: the dark shadow of the ecstasy itself.

We had three meetings at the Lutheran Centre and a large gathering at Guguletu township with ministers representing their churches. It was ten o'clock that evening when we at last arrived in Cape Town itself to stay in Archbishop Tutu's house, Bishopscourt. His wife Leah was there to welcome us but, sadly for me, Archbishop Desmond was in Europe for an international meeting. His absence from South Africa during my visit certainly robbed it of one, to me, crucial element; that of being welcomed home not only by the South African Council of Churches but by the Primate and Metropolitan of the Anglican Church itself. That celebration, however, must await the death and burial of apartheid. I hope I shall witness it in this world rather than the next.

Cape Town is a city built on the loveliest site in the world. Dominated by Table Mountain, sheltered, yet open to the converging Atlantic and Indian Oceans with the landmass of the whole of Africa behind it, its position is unique. Allister Spartis writes of it: 'When . . . "the black south-easter" . . . is not blowing and when the sun is shining on one of those still, crystal days that make the air tingle like champagne, the whole ambience of the Cape peninsula, with its grey-green slopes of mountain granite plunging steeply into a turquoise sea, is so translucently Mediterranean that it seems incredible it should have been bypassed by the southern Latins who were the first to land there, and left instead to Protestant northerners from the lowlands of Holland.'[19] Yet so it was. One strange consequence of its colonial history is that, in spite of its old Dutch houses, white-walled with red-tiled roofs, it has a strongly English feel to it. Oak trees are everywhere. On a rainy day, of which there are many, it could be somewhere on the Devon coast. And perhaps this accounts for its apparently sleepy and slow moving atmosphere: the very opposite of Johannesburg and the high-veldt that I know best.

My stay in Cape Town was short, just three days, but the programme arranged for me included three of the more significant visits of my whole three weeks' itinerary. The first was to the University of the Western Cape, one of the fastest growing universities in the country, embracing all the usual faculties but planning an Historical and Cultural Centre which will include a museum on the anti-apartheid era and an archive on the history of the South African liberation movement. This project, currently being supervised by Dr Andre Odendaal, and a focal point of the campus, will house the archive of the International Defence and Aid Fund. As chairman of the trustees of IDAF I wanted my visit to symbolize the transfer of this archive, including a beautiful handpainted transcription of the Freedom Charter itself which I handed over to the Rector, Professor Jakes Gerwel. Already more than 2000 films and videotapes, between 50,000 and 100,000 photographs and an entire range of publications on the history of the struggle have been shipped to Cape Town. It is in fact the biggest collection of its kind in the world. Some of the staff at IDAF in London, themselves South African exiles, will be working at this Centre and it is hoped that the museum and archive will form an integral part of a major new community-orientated multi-functional project completed stage by stage as funds become available.

It was exciting to be in such a university whose Chancellor is Archbishop Desmond Tutu and which is rapidly becoming a centre of excellence in the new South Africa. It was even more exciting to be contributing that unique archive, built up over thirty years and more, when every item in it had been banned and yet so carefully protected for future generations.

Included in my visit to the University was a journey through the vast area of squatter camps now spread out on the edge of the city. Their names are already known to the world because, so often, incidents of violence occur there as in Soweto, Tokoza, and the black townships of the Transvaal. Most notorious is Kwelitsha. I stood on a ridge overlooking that camp of some 350,000 people. It stretched to the far horizon, homes made of scrap metal, scrap timber, tarpaulins or corrugated iron and cardboard: anything to provide shelter. Its water supply, stand-pipes shared by hundreds of residents. Its sanitation, some form of bucket-system and the earth itself. As I was watching half a dozen small children ran up the slope to greet me, children no doubt who had known no other home except the shacks. Yet children with the 'shining morning face' of those ready and eager for the joy of playing together, and the equal joy of greeting strangers like myself with that marvellous smile of eyes and lips. Their clothes, however old and well worn, nevertheless were clean. And yet ... this, the largest of the many squatter camps of Cape Town, stretched not only to the far horizon but into the future of South Africa. Partly the consequence of removing four million people, partly the steady population growth, partly the pull of urbanisation and the supposed work opportunities it seems to offer. But *always* a challenge to the future and to any government that holds power in South Africa today. How can such a situation be met *soon*? How can the hope of providing for these hundreds of thousands of families a home worthy of their courage, their dignity and their joy become a reality before anger takes over from patience, violence from endurance?

On the final evening of my stay in Cape Town a great service of welcome was held in St George's Cathedral. I was told that nothing quite like it had been seen there before. It is a building that stands comparison with any Gothic church in any cathedral close in England. It certainly lends itself to the kind of ecclesiastical events that take place in all cathedrals on festive or civic or national occasions. It has seen the enthronement of many archbishops, the ordination of many priests, the baptism and confirmation of thousands of children through the years, over a century, since it was built. It is a cathedral greatly loved and greatly used not only by Anglicans but by many other denominations in these ecumenical days. Above all it is, as it has been for most of its history, a church expressing the meaning of the word 'catholic': *universal*. Multi-racial, multi-tribal, multi-cultural.

And on that night of my welcome it used music and song and dance in an outburst of joy. That was ecstasy. I find it indescribable in its spontaneity and grace. The 'marimba' is an African instrument which creates a special kind of rhythm not usually heard in cathedral music but, like the steel-band, irresistible. You cannot just listen to it, you are caught up into it. I wish Desmond Tutu could have been with me to share in it all.

I was to have had a morning of visits to other areas around Cape Town the next day, but I found myself quite drained of energy and cancelled the programme. I flew back to Johannesburg that afternoon.

*   *   *

I may have given the impression that the whole of my return visit to South Africa left no time for private socialising, focused as it was on the Conference and with its programme arranged by the African National Congress. It is true that there was not much. But for me there were individuals both black and white who had been so much a part of my life when I lived in Sophiatown and at St Peter's Rosettenville, that they had special priority. One of them was Olga Horowitz. When we first met, sometime in the early 1940s, Olga Price (as she was then, before her marriage to Charles Horowitz) was a journalist on *The Star*. At some point, and I now forget exactly when or why, I needed to reach the widest public I could. Television did not exist. Radio did, of course, but it was strictly controlled and censored by the government: increasingly so after the Nationalist Party came to power in 1948. *The Star* was the evening paper most widely read by the English-speaking sector in the Transvaal. So, to *The Star* offices I went with my story. It may well have been about the launching of the African Children's Feeding Scheme, but it was followed by so many other stories that I cannot now be sure which was the first. I was directed to Olga's desk in the large, open-plan reporters' room, and found her at her typewriter, fingers poised for action and (I am sure) a cigarette in her mouth. I was a chain smoker in those days and, as I recollect, all our interviews took place in a cloud of smoke. But what was unique about Olga was her ability to write her articles straight on to the typewriter. She never took notes and transcribed them later, her articles had an immediacy, an urgency, about them which made compelling reading. All I had to do was to tell the story. She would begin at once, pause occasionally to ask me a question, the exact spelling of a name, the description of a place, but there was never the need to explain the purpose of what I had come for. She was the most intuitive and sensitive journalist I have ever known. Without her I know I could not have reached across the barriers of racial prejudice or touched the hearts and minds (and pockets!) of the white community. Sometimes, coming back in the car from Pretoria or Roodeport or Krugersdorp, I would reach the outskirts of the city and find *Star* posters with banner headlines which I knew instantly to refer to my interview with Olga that morning. That could mean a massive mail of support for some project or other; it could equally well mean 'hate' telephone calls and abuse. But it always meant a heightening of public awareness on the issues which mattered most to us both.

We kept in touch through the years by post – always using pseudonyms on our airmail envelopes. In those long intervening years since 1956 we met occasionally in London. Her journalistic life at *The Star* still continued, and even after retirement she was recalled to write a daily article, 'Stoep Talk', which she still does.

I found her, now a widow, living in a beautiful tenth-floor flat with a view across Johannesburg. We simply talked as if we were still in that *Star* press-room (but neither of us smoking now!) about the politics of the present and the hopes of the future. We had a perfect dinner-party with just five or six friends, each one of them involved, intelligent, humane observers or activists in the fight for true democratic values, none of them stereotyped liberals or radicals. A few days after my return to England she wrote to me: 'The guest room is empty ... I don't have to tell you how marvellous your visit was for my heart and soul. We spoke a lot of ecstasy and agony. Have you yet encountered the agony of ecstasy? Do you recall the day you left when a man called Yousuf (an African) was supervising the putting up of curtains? When you left I heard loud sobbing. From Yousuf. Anxiously I got him to dry his tears. "I'm sorry. It's because I'm so elated", he said. "Never did I think I'd have the joy of welcoming Father Huddleston when he was all alone, not surrounded by crowds. What miracle brought me to this very place this very day to have his handshake?" What indeed? And what miracle brought you as my first house guest? I am also elated and feeling extraordinarily well.'

Ecstasy indeed, the agony of ecstasy.

*   *   *

> Day that I have loved, day that I have loved,
> The night is here . . .

In *Naught For Your Comfort* I used these lines from one of Rupert Brooke's poems to summarize my feelings over the destruction of Sophiatown, 'Something', I said, 'which cannot be built again so easily or so fair. When Sophiatown is finally obliterated and its people scattered, I believe that South Africa will have lost not only a place, but an ideal.'

In a strange way my last full day in the country brought back echoes, something more than memories, charged with the same foreboding, which have remained with me and will, I think, continue to reverberate in my mind.

I had received a message telling me that the political prisoners in Bophutatswana who were on hunger strike and in danger of death wanted to see me with Nelson Mandela. They were now in a hospital on the edge of Pretoria. Bophutatswana ('Bop' as it is usually called) is the 'homeland' nearest to Pretoria: its President Mangope, strongly supported by the South African government, is perhaps the most determined opponent of the ANC's policy of reincorporating the 'homelands' into the democratic South Africa of the future. The nationwide hunger strike of political prisoners had been taken up immediately by the ANC's supporters in 'Bop'. I was deeply moved at the request of these men and most anxious to see them. I was to be disappointed. Walter Sisulu, Abdul and I set off from Johannesburg and reached the hospital at about two o'clock. A small crowd of ANC supporters, relatives and friends of the hunger strikers, and others were awaiting us. Food was being cooked: songs were being sung: the black, green and gold of ANC flags were flying. It was a brilliant sunny winter day and the stubble was golden. The Transvaal high veldt was at its best.

We sat in the car and waited for Nelson to arrive: he had been on a visit somewhere and would arrive in Pretoria by charter plane. After an hour or so a message reached us to say that he was delayed: would we return to the Pretoria airport and await him there. By four o'clock we were introduced to government officials in the VIP lounge whose presence had been kept secret, amongst them a minister of state. This was to be my only direct contact with President de Klerk's government. We were received with courtesy, tea and sandwiches. After an hour or so we were told that Mandela's plane had taken off but it would be at least an hour before his arrival at Pretoria. Conversation was difficult. There were, we were told, 'problems' about our visit to the hunger strikers. President Mangope was a difficult man with whom to negotiate: there were delicate political issues involved . . . and so it went on.

At last Mandela arrived, shook hands with the Minister and said, 'I wish to see the hunger strikers'. But the Minister insisted that this was impossible without the approval of his superior, Mr Pik Botha, Minister of Foreign Affairs. He was travelling by car somewhere near Nelspruit and no telephonic communication was possible. It took nearly two hours before it was decided to phone directly to President de Klerk. Mandela's attitude was repeatedly summed up by the statement, 'I shall not leave here until I have seen the hunger strikers'. My view was the same, and I stated it quite clearly. When I was challenged by the Minister I said, 'As a bishop – or a priest, for that matter – if someone is dying and has asked to see me that request must take priority over

130

any other. I wish to stay.' But in fact, as Nelson told me, Oliver Tambo and other senior members of the ANC had arranged a farewell dinner for me in Johannesburg and it was already seven o'clock. Nelson requested me to go to that dinner and said he would convey my message to the men in hospital personally. I had no option but to do as he desired. There was for me no joy in the dinner party, either, for it was overshadowed by what was happening in Pretoria. In the event it was at two o'clock on the Sunday morning that Mandela was able to visit the men in hospital and persuade them to end their hunger strike with the promise that *all* political prisoners in 'Bop' would be released. It proved, as so often, a false promise. Mangope still holds scores of men as political prisoners and the de Klerk administration takes no steps to secure their release. The hunger strike goes on. The agony does, too.

When I finally left Johannesburg for London on Sunday evening it was Oliver Tambo who came to see me off, alone, just as it had been he who, in 1960, came to see me off, alone, on my sea journey to Tanzania. It is his friendship of nearly fifty years which is my greatest strength and consolation and the ground of my hope for the future of the African National Congress and so of South Africa.

9

Within three days of my return to England I was invited to address a public meeting at the headquarters of the Commonwealth Trust, sponsored by the Trust and the Anti-Apartheid Movement. The date was 18th July 1991. I am writing these words exactly three months later, and already what I said then is out of date. Such is the strange mingling of delay and pace in South Africa. Delay in implementing the promises made by President de Klerk over the release of prisoners, the return of exiles and the ending of violence; pace in the constant and determined movement by all parties to try to unite and co-ordinate their efforts to bring about the negotiating procedures on which peace itself depends. I have decided to publish extracts from that speech, which I described at the time as a provisional assessment of the situation I found, and a personal interpretation of it. I needed time to ponder what I had experienced before coming to any final position. Yet, after thee months, I find it even more difficult to give a clear and unambiguous answer to the simple question, asked of me a hundred times since my return: 'What is your view of the South African situation today?'

Here is my speech of 18th July, or at least the essential paragraphs from it; it is the spoken word. I shall end this book with a written word which will in some respects amend or even change the message I gave at that meeting.

It was ecstasy to be back, and I cannot begin to express it adequately, because of the absolute sincerity of the welcome – the depth of it, the strength of it, shown in a thousand different ways, through individuals whom I had known as schoolboys, now in their mid-fifties, to children I had never ever seen, who of course were just old enough to be my grandchildren, and who had never seen me or known me, but only heard of me. And so that kind of ecstasy is something for which I can only say that I thank God, because without anything else, it has made my life worth living . . .

It was a tremendous experience for me to be there and to have had the honour of being asked to open the conference of the African National Congress, and to speak in my opening address to the theme of the Conference – a terrific responsibility, but entrusted to me. I could never forget that and if I never have any other such experience I shall be more than content with that . . .

Take hold of this because it is very important for the future: the African National Congress is now in a position to lead from strength internally. Of course, it has always been in this position, as you saw in February of last year, when the whole country was covered in black, green and yellow flags – you could see the strength of the ANC which had survived all those years of repression and horror and devastation. But today it is there in strength, in commitment and in unity and it has got tremendous leadership . . .

I want to remind you of the basis of all this, which it is necessary for us to remember. It comes in the Declaration of that special session of the United Nations in December 1989 – the Declaration on South Africa which was unanimously agreed by all countries, including the USA and Great Britain. Whether reluctantly or not they agreed this resolution and it reads as follows: 'To ensure that the international community does not relax existing measures aimed at encouraging the South African regime to eradicate apartheid, *until there is clear evidence of profound and irreversible change* – bearing in mind the objectives of this Declaration.'

That 'profound and irreversible change' can only come about when, first of all, there is an all-party conference embracing all parties in South Africa, whose representatives are not chosen by President de Klerk or the present Government but are freely elected, an all-party conference which then decides on the parameters of constitutional change which will lead to an interim government before the negotiating process can really start. Because, as I hope you realize, President de Klerk has never gone back on his promise to his own electorate that the present Government of South Africa will remain in office and will fix the agenda for the negotiations, and that he will be the chairman of that negotiating process. This is still his firm and *prepared* intention, and it is not acceptable to the ANC or any other of the bodies who have been taking part in the struggle. It cannot come about this way. You have to have an interim government, freely elected, in place. And that has to lead on to something like a constituent assembly which will eventually set up the democratic process for free and fair elections. None of this has happened. When President Bush declares that some progress has been made, that now is the time to lift all sanctions, to repeal the anti-apartheid law in the States, he must know that there is no question at this moment of 'fundamental and irreversible change'. And that is not to deny hope. I am not an optimist because optimism is useless in this situation, but I am hopeful, and I will dare to declare that I will see apartheid dead and buried before I am. I said this repeatedly in South Africa so I might as well say it again: I am now in my seventy-ninth year, and I told the ANC and everybody else, 'You had better get a move on!'

I believe that de Klerk has three years at the most in which to provide for a new constitution, for democratic processes and for a freely-elected, non-racial, democratic parliament. He has three years because the one thing that is irreversible is the fact that he cannot conceivably go back to the old electoral system. That is gone for ever . . .

The question is whether, during these next few years or so, the international community together with the forces of change inside South Africa – not only the ANC, but COSATU (the trade union movement), the PAC, Inkatha itself and all other organisations which will be around that negotiating table, working together with the international community – whether they can keep up the pressure on de Klerk. That is your responsibility and my responsibility . . .

The Anti-Apartheid Movement will go on and will do everything possible to meet the challenge that Nelson Mandela has made to us, to make certain that the conscience of the world is kept alive by the AAM. He emphasizes this over and over again, and I will quote his own words to end with: 'We are calling for flexibility and for imagination, appropriately realistic; but our position is very clear: sanctions must continue to be maintained and applied. That is our position. The flexibility we want exercised is intended to ensure that this weapon is kept in our hands.'

The two most important events which have taken place since I made that speech are what is now known as 'The Inkatha-gate scandal' and all the unsavoury revelations of collusion and the funding of the Inkatha Freedom Party by the South African Government; and the Peace Accord signed by President de Klerk, Nelson Mandela and Gatsha Buthelezi, together with some twenty other organisations, religious and secular, and representing the vast majority of the population. I have already spoken of these two events though they took place after I had left the country. Their impact is still to be fully felt. The proper control of the violence will be the proof of the effectiveness of the Peace Accord, but that will depend greatly on whether President de Klerk has the authority to control his own security forces.

Nelson Mandela, ever since he walked out of Pollsmoor

Prison, has asserted again and again that de Klerk is 'a man of integrity'. He has said this because he believes it. And he is in the strongest position to make such a judgment because of his close and private contact with the President. But this has not prevented him, in recent weeks, publicly and strongly attacking de Klerk for his failure to control the security forces and his refusal to accept that the violence has its origin in some kind of 'third force' whose sole objective is to destabilize the country by undermining the credibility of the ANC.

What does 'integrity' mean?

It can be said, and I would be certainly prepared to say it, that Mikhail Gorbachev is 'a man of integrity', 'someone I can do business with', in Margaret Thatcher's phrase. Yet Gorbachev was born and bred in a Marx-Leninist Communist society. He knew no other. When he instituted his reforms by 'glasnost' and 'perestroika' six years ago, he had no intention of rejecting the ideology in which he fully believed. He simply thought that it needed correction, and that he had the power to correct it. He continued to think that way until the attempted coup by Communist hard-liners and the army almost succeeded in ending his own life as well as his country's hopes. The consequences of that error of judgment will be with the world for decades to come, and who can be sure of the outcome?

President de Klerk was born and bred in a strictly orthodox Afrikaner family which believed absolutely in white supremacy – that is white racism – and in the ideology of apartheid which expresses that ideology in law, custom and political allegiance. De Klerk has spent his entire political life in the Nationalist Party, thirteen years of it as a cabinet minister. He has in fact been responsible for enforcing the apartheid laws, more particularly the worst of them, the Bantu Education Act, for he was Minister of Education before he became President. As we have seen, he has never 'repented' of apartheid nor denounced it as evil. He has simply said – and, to be fair, acted on his words – that it was 'a mistake'. What I am asserting is that Gorbachev and de Klerk are 'men of integrity' *within* the ideologies which they have been born into, and from which I believe neither man has escaped. This is one reason why I am not an optimist about the present transitional period in South African history. Optimism, like patriotism, is 'not enough'. But *hope* is enough, because it is based on realism. Ultimately, for the religious believer, it is based on the truth (as we accept it) that this is God's world and not ours. For the Christian believer it is also based on the fundamental truth that God has Himself entered this world, has been 'enfleshed' in our common humanity and has therefore given to every person an infinite and changeless dignity.

Whatever view we take of President de Klerk's integrity, or, for that matter, Nelson Mandela's, it is now obvious that the transition from institutionalized racism, apartheid, to democracy and its institution is going to be a period of intense turbulence. We need hope, not optimism, if we are to help South Africa realize its freedom.

It has also already become obvious that the transitional period will be a struggle for political *power*, which history shows to be full of ethical and moral dangers. African countries (like all other countries seeking national identity), since achieving political independence from their colonial masters, have all seen just how dangerous power can be. South Africa will not be the exception.

The African National Congress and its leadership has

the immense privilege and opportunity of showing the world that it at least has learnt the lesson.

So long as it regards itself as the representative of the voiceless millions of its supporters in the towns and villages of the country; so long as it stands by the principles expressed in the Freedom Charter; so long as it is not deceived by the enticements of Western capitalism masquerading as democracy itself: it will reach the end of its 'golden string', and be led in 'at the golden gate built in Jerusalem's wall' – the golden gate of true fulfilment, peace and liberty.

NOTES

1 *Southern Africa Review of Books*, Feb/Mar 1990.
2 Worsnip, Michael E, *Between the Two Fires* University of Natal Press, 1991, pp 74–5.
3 Scott, Michael *A Time to Speak* London, 1958, p 55.
4 Ibid, p 150.
5 Chikane, Frank, *No Life of My Own* (CIIR) 1988.
6 *New Statesman* 27th September 1991.
7 Sparks, Allister, *The Mind of South Africa* (Heinemann, London).
8 Benson, Mary, *Nelson Mandela* (Penguin Books, London, 1986), p 67.
9 Ibid.
10 Willan, Brian, *Sol Plaatje* (Heinemann, London, 1984).
11 Ibid.
12 Ibid.
13 Ibid.
14 Quoted by Brian Willan in *Sol Plaatje*.
15 Ibid.
16 Ibid.
17 Luthuli, Albert, *Let My People Go* (Johannesburg, 1962), p 152.
18 Gracie (ed), *Gandhi and Charlie* (Cowley Publications, Cambridge, Massachusetts, 1989).
19 Sparks, Allister, *The Mind of South Africa*.